# LIBERTY AND ORDER IN EARLY MODERN EUROPE

# STUDIES IN MODERN HISTORY

General editors: *John Morrill and David Cannadine*

This series, intended primarily for students, will tackle significant historical issues in concise volumes which are both stimulating and scholarly. The authors combine a broad approach, explaining the current state of our knowledge in the area, with their own research and judgements; and the topics chosen range widely in subject, period and place.

*Titles already published*

# LIBERTY AND ORDER IN EARLY MODERN EUROPE

## The subject and the State, 1650–1800

*J. H. Shennan*

**LONGMAN**
London and New York

LONGMAN GROUP LIMITED
Longman House, Burnt Mill, Harlow
Essex CM20 2JE, England
*Associated companies throughout the world*

*Published in the United States of America
by Longman Inc., New York*

*First published 1986*

BRITISH LIBRARY CATALOGUING IN PUBLICATION DATA

Shennan, J. H.
    Liberty and order in early modern Europe,
    1650–1800.–(Studies in modern history)
    1. Europe–History–1648–1789
    I. Title    II. Series
    940.2′5         D273

ISBN 0-582-49464-8

LIBRARY OF CONGRESS CATALOGING IN PUBLICATION DATA

Shennan, J. H.

    Liberty and order in early modern Europe, 1650–1800.
    (Studies in modern history)
    Bibliography: p.
    Includes index.
    1. Europe–Politics and government–1648–1789.
I. Title.    II. Series: Studies in modern history
(Longman (Firm))
JN9.S49    1986        940.2′5        85–23075

ISBN 0-582-49464-8

Set in 10/11pt Linotron Times
Produced by Longman Group (FE) Limited
Printed in Hong Kong

# CONTENTS

# PROLOGUE

In the long continuum of human history the state is a latecomer upon the scene. Yet over a relatively brief time-scale it has become the supreme object of allegiance, before which even ties of blood and friendship have to be sacrificed. Its emergence has fundamentally and universally transformed human values and relationships. The idea of an impersonal state commanding the ultimate loyalty of governments and subjects alike is one of the most elusive themes to emerge from a study of early modern European history. It is difficult to fix a precise time-scale for the progress of this concept, though few would deny that in our own generation it has come to dominate our lives. These facts oblige the historian to ask when such an idea was first mooted and how it began to acquire such potency.

In an earlier essay I attempted to chart the origins of the modern impersonal state in Europe in the period between 1500 and the early eighteenth century. The growing power of princely government at the beginning of that period led to a general crisis stretching from the mid-sixteenth to the mid-seventeenth century. At the heart of this protracted struggle, as the power of the prince was being transformed and reshaped, was the issue of sovereignty, the question of where, in the last resort, legitimate political authority resided. Despite the variety of socio-economic and political structures involved, the direction which countries followed in the aftermath of that crisis pointed universally, if unevenly, towards the concept of the abstract state.[1]

This present work takes as its starting point the period around 1650, though it is predominantly concerned with the eighteenth century. It ends with the maelstrom of Revolutionary Europe but does not draw any conclusions about the new political order which emerged from the turmoil. Its subject once more is the pursuit of the impersonal state idea, and the approach again that of juxtaposing political ideas and political practices in the expectation that each

vii

sphere will illumine the other. By this period, however, as the concept of the abstract state becomes clearer, a new, though closely related subject, forces itself into the reckoning. The question of what limits may be properly imposed by the power of the state upon the liberty of the subject, or whether indeed the subject's liberty is simply a gift of the state, began to loom larger before the end of the eighteenth century, and such questions have grown in importance ever since. This volume is equally concerned, therefore, with the nature of the relationship between state control and political freedom.

Man's quest for political freedom has been one of the major themes underlying the writing of history, at least in the West, for the past two hundred years. That doughty controversialist, J. H. Hexter, recently castigated English historians of Tudor and Stuart politics writing since the 1930s for not recognizing its pre-eminent importance and for thus failing, in his words, 'to know first things first'.[2] In pointing up the perceived eccentricity of latterday scholarship, such criticism merely emphasizes the alternative normality. Whether Professor Hexter's strictures are well-founded is a side issue so far as this essay is concerned. However, he has performed a service by reminding historians that they should from time to time re-examine such dominant themes, especially when they remain an essential element in contemporary debate.

One of the difficulties is that the nature of this political freedom defies precise definition. 'Like happiness and goodness, like nature and reality', comments Isaiah Berlin, 'the meaning of this term is so porous that there is little interpretation that it seems able to resist.'[3] Hexter's definition does not help to resolve the problem. For him liberty depends upon the existence of 'assemblies of representatives freely elected from constituencies geographically defined'. However, the link between the institutional arrangements for government and the power of the state to enforce its decisions upon all subjects, supporters and opponents alike, remains obscure, particularly in the early modern period with which Hexter is mainly concerned. There were no efficient dictatorships in early modern Europe, and it is at least arguable that political liberty could survive as well under an inefficient absolutist regime like that of France as under a rather more efficient representative government like that of England.

In fact, the pursuit of political liberty for the individual is an ideal of relatively recent origin, with no roots in the ancient or medieval world. It was in the long crisis of the early modern period that the search for political order and security was first expressed in the coded language of liberty. Since then that language has remained central to explanations of historical change and of man's experience in modern society. In this generation we continue to divide the world into the oppressed and the free, and East and West, we invest the word 'democracy' with precisely opposed meanings, according to which side of the fence, or perhaps more accurately in this context, the Wall, we establish our ideological position.

Indeed, liberty and security are two concepts which the historian can scarcely examine apart, and the final question to be explored in this volume is whether the reality of recent human experience may have been distorted by an emphasis upon the former rather than upon the latter.

Perhaps the subject matter of this work may be summarized in the form of a musical metaphor. It is a set of variations upon a theme. The theme is a complex one, composed for two linked motifs, the one the growth of the abstract state and the other the increase or the loss of liberty experienced by the subject in the light of that growth. The first motif is in the major key; and the development from the princely towards the impersonal state establishes the piece's dominant form and tone. The second is in the minor. Its development is less assured, more mysterious than that of its major counterpart: for does liberty give way to order as the state's power grows or does order salvage freedom from anarchy? The variations which follow the initial statement of this elaborate theme explore the manner in which the relationship between the two motifs is affected by the differing structures and traditions of Europe. France and Russia have been chosen to represent the fundamental division between West and East, though the conclusions arrived at from a study of these two countries have been supplemented by contrasting or comparable evidence available from some of their respective neighbours.

And how, finally, should we respond to the work in performance? That rather depends upon the ear of the listener, for this particular work is fraught with ambiguity. When Beethoven gave musical expression to Goethe's drama, the tragedy of *Egmont*, a quarter of a century after the outbreak of the French Revolution, he evoked a spirit of freedom with which many West European listeners could joyfully identify, an ideal of personal liberty characteristic of the German *Aufklärung*. But such a reaction was unlikely to be universal. And even where the response was enthusiastic there could be no escaping the fact that Count Egmont's defence of freedom on behalf of the Netherlands ultimately proved to be irreconcilable with the needs of the established political order in Madrid. His dilemma has been handed on, unresolved, to trouble the contemporary world.

This prologue has established our three related themes: the emergence of the concept of the abstract state, the nature of the subjects' liberty vis-à-vis state power, and the question of whether the relationship between that power and that liberty has been correctly interpreted by historians and other commentators. These themes will be variously explored in the following chapters. In the first chapter political ideas tending to be the emergence of the concept of impersonal statehood will be examined, particularly that tendency to perceive subjects as individuals rather than as members of well-defined groups. It was in England, towards the close of the seventeenth century, that such ideas first came close to mirroring political practice. The central section of Chapter 1, therefore, will be concerned with Britain seen as a touchstone for comparison with other countries in Europe, where developments in the direction of abstract statehood were taking place. Britain is significant, too, as a forum for the discussion of the nature of liberty, especially economic liberty, within the framework of powerfully centralized political control. Finally, the role of eighteenth-century history writing has to be added to the reckoning. For its evolutionary thrust, perceived by some, like Vico and Gibbon, in terms of the rise and decline of societies, and by others, like Condorcet, of irresistible human progress, fed a growing preoccupation with the rival claims of order and liberty. Its effect overall was to inculcate a view of history characterized by the quest for freedom of one sort or another.

Chapters 2–4 will be concerned chiefly with France, though they will also contain comparative sections on her western and southern neighbours, Britain, the United Provinces, and especially the Bourbon kingdom of Spain. The powerful bonds which united the French crown and its nobility inhibited the emergence of the abstract state idea. The privileges granted to separate corporate groups, the nobility in particular, constituted their liberties. Liberty as a universal concept, on the other hand, was an idea that only began to provoke public discussion from the second half of the eighteenth century. That discussion inevitably entailed the concept of equality as well. There were attractions in this concept for the French crown, particularly the possibility of being able to levy taxation universally. Yet despite some indications to the contrary, its authority ultimately remained too deeply bound to the *status quo* to allow it to act on behalf of an impersonal ideal, or even of a new kind of moral order, the French state.

Chapters 5 and 6 will be concerned with Muscovy and the Russian Empire. In contrast to the western world the political order in seventeenth-century Muscovy knew neither the concept of liberty nor of liberties. Equality, conversely, was recognized in the equal subordination to the tsar of all his subjects. Peter the Great sought to build upon this authoritarian, religious-based tradition to establish a secular regime of service to an abstract state. However, his successors were unable to sustain this ideal. Instead, a new noble class emerged in eighteenth-century Russia, with a set of formally prescribed privileges or liberties of a kind familiar in Western Europe. Paradoxically, this 'contractual' relationship between the ruler and the nobility was established in Russia at precisely the time in the West when it was being undermined by demands for universal liberty and

equality. The Russian world, with its extremes of liberty and subjection, represented by the figures of the cossack and the serf,
provides a particularly instructive setting for the examination of our
themes. By the end of the eighteenth century Russian writers themselves were beginning to debate the relative claims to priority of
political freedom and security.

In the final chapter the canvas will be widened to embrace a
consideration of Russia's neighbours to the west and north: Poland,
Sweden and the German states. Despite some similarities with
Russia, Poland developed a regime which was totally dominated by
the nobility. The absolute priority that they demanded for their
corporate liberties at the expense of the crown, and of a population
which was for the most part enserfed, fatally undermined the
security of the state itself. Sweden, on the other hand, moved closer
than any other country with the exception of Britain to abstract
statehood. The governing tradition of constitutional checks and
balances, and of emphasis upon the supremacy of the law, enabled
her to avoid the twin polarities of unrestrained liberty and absolute
servitude. Finally, in examining aspects of the German Enlightenment of the eighteenth century, the *Aufklärung*, we are once more
reminded of the importance for our subject of the role played by
history and history writing. For the historians of the German, as of
the French and British Enlightenment, freedom was to be discovered in the evolution of political societies. German writers also
began to enunciate the idea that the state itself was a moral force
and the only setting in which subjects could aspire to achieve full
liberty. Before the end of the eighteenth century that idea was being
expressed by non-German writers too. It seemed to offer the only
means of reconciling the conflicting demands of liberty for the
subject and security for the state.

*[handwritten margin note: State as moral force]*

## REFERENCES AND NOTES

1. J. H. Shennan, *The Origins of the Modern European State,
   1450–1725* (London 1974). A number of other books dealing
   with aspects of the same theme have appeared since that date.
   They include Kenneth Dyson, *The State Tradition in Western
   Europe* (Oxford 1980); Nannerl O. Keohane, *Philosophy and
   the State in France* (Princeton 1980); Theodore K. Rabb, *The
   Struggle for Stability in Early Modern Europe* (Oxford 1975);
   and Herbert H. Rowen, *The King's State: proprietary
   dynasticism in early modern France* (New Brunswick 1980).
2. J. H. Hexter, 'The birth of modern freedom', *Times Literary
   Supplement*, 21 Jan 1983.
3. Isaiah Berlin, *Four Essays on Liberty* (Oxford 1969), p. 121.

# ACKNOWLEDGEMENTS

I have been assisted by a number of people and institutions in the completion of this book. I am indebted to the University of Lancaster for maintaining in difficult times its enlightened attitude to study leave; to the Master and Fellows of Corpus Christi College, Cambridge, for inviting me to return as a Senior Research Scholar; to the Twenty-Seven Foundation for generous financial support. The editors of this series, John Morrill and David Cannadine, both offered most helpful criticism of the book's first draft and deserve much credit for its revised form. As always my wife's assistance has been crucial throughout, both in the structuring of the book and in the formulation of the argument. All these people have helped me to produce an improved final version, though none bears responsibility for remaining errors or for the interpretation.

**For Chris**

Leviathan lives and moves before our eyes, all the more dangerous because in infancy he was called liberty.

(A. B. Cobban, *In Search of Humanity*, 1960)

*Chapter one*

# CHANGING INTELLECTUAL PATTERNS

## THE DEBATE BEGINS: PRIVATE RIGHTS VERSUS PUBLIC AUTHORITY

The European political order in the late fifteenth and sixteenth centuries was brittle, the threat of anarchy pressing and ever-present. Europe existed on the edge of chaos as civil war became endemic in different parts of the continent: the English Wars of the Roses, the Castilian War of Succession, the French Wars of Religion, Muscovy's Time of Troubles. These episodes were manifestations of a universal malaise as those leaders of the pack, the princes, fought to replace the outmoded diarchy of Pope and Emperor and the sundered chain of feudal command. In the frenzied search for order they were constantly forced to make new demands on their subjects, demands which had the effect of blurring the public and private roles of both ruler and subject in joint recognition of the supreme importance of security. With such developments, powerfully supported by the voices of Machiavelli, Castiglione and the other so-called mirror-for-prince theorists, we may discern the first, though still distant portents of the modern state idea.[1]

Security, like liberty is an elusive concept, and one that has developed dramatically since the heyday of dynastic kingship. It is not necessarily the antithesis of liberty though it may be; certainly, all who have benefited from it have had to accept some limitation upon their freedom of action. It has always tended to represent the point of balance between the government's exercise of *force majeure* and the self-interest of the subject, though that fine point will vary according to prevailing political, social, economic and ideological mores. It is most commonly perceived today as the ultimate justification for the exercise of state power, applied universally to the citizenry. However, in early modern Europe there could be no such universality of treatment since relationships between government and governed depended upon group interests and not upon the aspirations of individuals. There is a need for caution, therefore, lest the concept of the impersonal state be brought prematurely to birth.

1

That it is possible to anticipate the emergence of the impersonal state idea owes much to the work of the sixteenth-century French political theorist, Jean Bodin. This has been subjected to a subtle and penetrating analysis by Dr Howell Lloyd, who maintains that Bodin did indeed grasp and enunciate the idea of the state as a distinct entity, subsisting in its own right.[2] Whether such an idea can co-exist in more than embryonic form with that of a society specifically defined in terms of inequality – any more than Leonardo da Vinci's design for a submarine could be usefully developed in a pre-technological environment – remains the crucial question. Bodin himself began his *Six livres de la république*, published in 1576, with a reminder of the unequal basis upon which his political order was posited, by introducing the analogy of the family. For Bodin families consisted of husband and wife, father and child, master and servant, owner and slave. Only the head of a family would become a political activist, 'leaving his family to enter into a city, and his domestic affairs to entreat of public; and instead of a lord, calleth himself a citizen'. Bodin emphasized an elitist political order which seemed to him always certain to triumph even over Platonic ideals of equality: 'There was never commonwealth, were it true or but imaginery, or the most popular that a man could think of; where the citizens were equal in all rights and prerogatives; but that always some of them have had more or less than others.'[3] It is difficult to invoke the awesome and universal sovereignty of the modern state on the basis of this essentially contractual relationship between one group of subjects and their preferred government.

To speak in terms of contractual sovereignty, however, rather than of state power, is not to deny the government's independence in post-Renaissance Europe from the various property-owning groups to whom it was contracted. The mystique of government tended to create the sense of separate identity necessary to command universal obedience, a process furthered by increasing institutional complexity. In early modern Europe urgent need, born out of threats to security, forced governments to demand adjustments to their contracts. Thus the ground was prepared for nurturing the idea of an impersonal state to which all had ultimately to defer, government and governed. The full development of that idea depended not only upon the growing power of government but also upon a profound shift in the nature of the relationship between government and society. In the words of another recent analyst of Bodin's thought, 'It is above all the notion of the citizen as an individual and not as a member of an estate, corporation or community which makes possible a fully fledged concept of the state.'[4]

It remained possible for some time, therefore, to challenge the 'must' of public need with the 'ought' of private morality. Sixteenth-century lawyers fought to defend the sanctity of private property

2

from governmental trespass save, in the phrase of the French jurist, Du Moulin, 'when the common good and the necessity of the public weal requires it.'[5] Even this proviso was considered too indulgent across the Channel, where since the thirteenth century the English Parliament had been establishing the principle that compulsory acquisition of property *per legem terrae* had to be accompanied by adequate payment of compensation, independently assessed. True there was a later continental legal tradition which the father of international law, the Dutchman Hugo Grotius, was to sum up early in the seventeenth century when he asserted that the taking of property without cause and compensation was contrary to natural law.[6] By then, however, Europe was in the throes of that interstate conflict known as the Thirty Years War, which strengthened the claims of governments to exercise the unlimited powers of *raison d'état*. Indeed, in the opinion of Theodore K. Rabb, the consequence of this climactic struggle was 'the conclusive establishment of the structure that is recognizable as the modern state, organized around an impersonal, centralized and unifying system of government, resting on law, bureaucracy and force'.[7]

In the spectrum of the seventeenth century that observation is not universally applicable. However, it is true that in that age the social and political nature of man, rather than his group rights and responsibilities, began to interest European philosophers. The reasons are difficult to determine. No doubt they include the fact that government was so enlarging its areas of intervention as to leave the subjects increasingly uncertain of why and how far they must support its authority and policies. Also the belief in divine right kingship was being undermined by scientific attitudes and observations which cast doubt upon the validity of the conventional Thomist cosmology, that view of the Christian universe which, since the time of St Thomas Aquinas, had been the official teaching of the Church. If the Earth was not at the centre of the universe, and the universe was of infinite vastness, what certainty could there be that God was so immediately concerned with the political organization of his people?[8]

Then in 1637, René Descartes published his brief *Discours de la méthode*. Its opening sentence sounds a note no less striking and challenging than that of Rousseau's *Du contrat social*: 'Good sense is of all things in the world the most evenly distributed'; and he continues, 'the power of judging rightly, and of distinguishing what is true from what is false, which is generally called good sense or reason, is equal by nature in all men'. Thus, in the words of R. J. White, Descartes 'proclaimed the essential basis of democracy: the natural intellectual equality of man in the courts of reason'.[9] It was a potentially devastating doctrine in a world regulated by hierarchy, a doctrine reinforced by the philosopher's central proposition, 'Je pense, donc je suis', from which he concluded that man was a 'thinking thing', as he defined him later, in the *Méditations* of 1641.[10]

A decade later Hobbes began his *Leviathan* with a section entitled 'Of Man', thereby confirming the Cartesian principle of equality, though less in the courts of reason than in the sovereign's court. Unlike Bodin, Hobbes chose to relegate differences of status between the subjects to an inconsequential level and to emphasize the fundamental equality upon which the political order was founded:

> For in the sovereignty is the fountain of honour. The dignities of lord, earl, duke and prince are his creatures. As in the presence of the master, the servants are equal, and without any honour at all; so are the subjects, in the presence of the sovereign. And though they shine some more, some less, when they are out of his sight; yet in his presence, they shine no more than the stars in presence of the sun.[11]

Such an approach also led Hobbes to stress the public 'must' at the expense of the private 'ought', the security of the state at the expense of individual liberty. Indeed, his chapter entitled, 'Of the Liberty of Subjects' reads rather like a justification for the opposite. Nor is that surprising since Hobbes viewed the subjects' liberty as no more than their recognition of the primacy of security. Hence the warning that men might be deceived 'by the specious name of Liberty'; and hence his preferred perspective: 'The end of obedience is protection'; and again, 'in the act of our submission, consisteth both our obligation, and our liberty'.[12] Thus he was less concerned to define those occasions upon which the public power might trespass upon private property than to assert that the latter depended exclusively upon the former's validation. Paradoxically it was beginning to appear that when man rather than groups of men became the central concern of political philosophy, the equality which resulted was likely to be of subjection to an ever more irresistible idea, that of the impersonal state.

However, that other great political philosopher of seventeenth-century England, John Locke, offered a different interpretation. He was not disposed, of course, to deny the centrality of human experience, nor man's essential equality: 'Thus we are born free, as we are born rational', he observed in his second *Treatise of Government*, composed in the 1680s. In his view political society arose out of the interplay of these two attributes common to all mankind. He argued that

> The Freedom, then, of man and liberty of acting according to his own will, is grounded on his having reason, which is able to instruct him in that law he is to govern himself by, and make him know how far he is left to the freedom of his own will. To turn him loose to an unrestrained liberty, before he has reason to guide him, is not the allowing him the privilege of his nature, to be free; but to thrust him out amongst brutes, and abandon him to a state as wretched, and as much beneath that of a man, as theirs.[13]

In other words, with maturity man becomes, in the Cartesian phrase, 'a thinking thing', distinguishable thereby from all other substances on this planet.

But Locke did not choose to follow Hobbes' emphasis upon the power of the state – that great Leviathan. Instead he preferred to stress man's right to life, liberty and property as the only matters with which governments should concern themselves. His emphasis upon property rights united him to an older legal tradition and provided a respectable justification for the establishment of political power. For the preservation of liberties – in the ownership of property which in its extended Lockean sense included life, possessions and pre-rogatives – provided a moral basis for the exercise of political power which was singularly lacking in Hobbes' state, his 'Artificial Man'. Locke, who had reached manhood at the beginning of the Interreg-num and rejoiced at the restoration of Charles II in 1660, was by the beginning of the 1680s concerned to refute the doctrine of absolutism. He was disinclined, therefore, to pay much attention to the idea of sovereignty even though it was implicit in his own acceptance of the fundamental equality of *homo sapiens* in the politi-cal equation. Yet his alternative was illusory: the defence of property could no longer be seen as part of the contract between the crown on the one hand and the owners of property (however widely interpre-ted) on the other. The English polity had grown far too complex for that. The location of sovereignty was buried in the mutual rela-tionship between crown, lords and commons whence it provided the inner force by which the outward forms were maintained. Whether or not these outward forms marked, as Professor MacPherson has famously insisted, the triumph of possessive individualism in Eng-land, they were certainly given great weight and significance by the underlying concept of state sovereignty which was becoming estab-lished in England after the Revolution of 1688.[14]

## THEORY AND PRACTICE IN BRITAIN

The signs of the appearance of state sovereignty were manifold. The Bank of England, established in 1694, provided a public stimulus to the nation's economic development, and a firm surety for its inter-national commitments. At the same time a fundamental change took place in the attitude towards public service, accompanied by a huge increase in government personnel. In the words of Geoffrey Holmes, 'By 1730 . . . there flourished in England a substantial body of pro-fessionals who were directly employed by the state either in civil office or in the armed forces and whose vocational justification lay entirely in serving the state's needs.'[15] As a result of the growth in central government authority in the 1680s, and of the decades of war against Louis XIV which followed, both the army and the navy grew to an unprecedented size, and the signs were that each had also attained a new level of professional competence and public recognition. An accepted pattern of promotion in the Navy began to be discerned, while a system of half-pay for regular army officers was introduced during peacetime.

These developments required the creation of an efficient infrastructure to support them. A permanent civil bureaucracy began to emerge, characterized by increasing specialization and departmentalism, in the service of governments whose effective cabinet structure tended to obscure the nature of royal authority. Even written and oral entrance examinations were introduced into parts of the civil service, a striking illustration of the growth of impersonal public service. Matching changes took place in the foreign department. British diplomats abroad no longer communicated directly with the king but with the secretary of state and their careers became more regularized in terms of salary, promotion and retirement pensions.

Most significant of all was the power of parliamentary statute, the true voice of sovereignty. That voice spoke strongly for the landed and propertied interests, but it was nevertheless the universal public arbiter, its pronouncements no longer to be confused with the contracted benefits of a particular privileged group. Though such measures as the draconian game laws of the eighteenth century testify to the determination of the social and political establishment to protect the owners of property, there is another side to that coin which suggests a more subtle appreciation of the wider obligations of political authority. So long as poaching did not assume the proportions of organized robbery, the game laws, in the words of a reforming Member of Parliament, John Curwen, 'had not been executed with their utmost vigour'.[16] Even so, by the end of the eighteenth century, Parliament was ready to debate their reform precisely on the grounds that they smacked of exclusivity which was no longer defensible in the national interest. The Game Reform Act was finally passed in 1831. Similarly, the authorities' unwillingness to put down eighteenth-century bread riots with force was a tacit recognition of the state's obligation, in times of dearth, to prevent bread prices from climbing too steeply.[17]

In eighteenth-century Britain political ideas reflected the outlook of a community secularized and refined by the subtlety of its civic relationships and distanced from that primitive urge to self-preservation which more evidently characterized less highly developed societies. Security remained the overwhelming need. But when it was sought within the framework of an advanced and elaborate polity, the irresistible sovereign will which guaranteed it could be concealed behind private claims to liberty and property.

Adam Ferguson, whose *Essay on the History of Civil Society* was published in 1767, put the matter thus: 'mankind having laid the basis of safety, proceed to erect a superstructure suitable to their views.'[18] Ferguson was Professor of Moral Philosophy in the University of Edinburgh, and it was among the great figures of the Scottish Enlightenment that the political ideas of John Locke were most powerfully developed and criticized in the second half of the eighteenth century.

By the time that Adam Ferguson was writing, ideas of liberty and property had been joined by the novel concept of progress. In late-eighteenth-century Britain the pursuit of literary and scientific arts reflected the burgeoning commercial prosperity which in turn mirrored, in the division of labour, the growing complexity of society. It also seemed reasonable to assume that a powerful, prosperous and expansive regime would enjoy a greater degree of security than one narrowly based on militarism. In such a progressive order, however, divisions between rich and poor were likely to grow, thereby raising questions about the kind of relationship which existed between the citizens and the government, and about the nature of their liberty. Ferguson sought to answer these questions.

If citizens were not perceived as possessing a basic political equality then the concept of state sovereignty could not endure. Ferguson was certain that they did, but only in a very limited sense: they all possessed an equal right to defend themselves. The transmission of that right by the state to all citizens constituted their essential liberty: 'Security in fact, is the essence of freedom.' This was the Hobbesian view restated: 'in the act of our submission consisteth both our obligation, and our liberty.' Beyond that limited equality Ferguson had no illusion about the predominantly unequal nature of civil society in eighteenth-century Britain: 'In respect to sex and age, strength of body and mind, individuals are destined to inequality from their birth; and, almost in the first steps of society, bear the distinctions which industry and courage give in the different attainments of men, and lead in the sequel to all the varieties of profession and fortune.' He then argued that that natural inequality helped to account for the acceptability of a sovereignty which, while guaranteeing security for all citizens, in every other respect discriminated hugely between them. He argued that it was impossible and undesirable to resist the effects of birth, ability, education, property and station in the distinctive ranking of citizens: 'In these inequalities we find the first germ of subordination and government so necessary to the safety of individuals and the peace of mankind; and in these also we find the continued incentive to labour and the practice of lucrative arts.'[19] In other words, the exploitation of commercial opportunity, a theme associated in particular with the work of Ferguson's countryman and academic contemporary, Adam

Smith, depended upon the universal recognition of the state's sovereignty, which in turn forced the subjects to make the most of their own advantages.

Although there can be no denying the ultimate priority given by Ferguson to the needs of security – 'the felicity of nations is proportioned to the degree in which every citizen is safe'[20] his enthusiastic belief in progress somewhat obscured that primary consideration since by implication advanced societies were less preoccupied with martial matters than with the pacific pursuit of commerce and with triumphs in the arts and sciences. Indeed at one point he goes so far as to suggest that modern warfare was little more than a stylized version of the original, which could be managed and limited by common-sensical human beings: 'We are, in this respect, certainly more happy in modern times. War is made with little national animosity, and battles are fought without any personal exasperation of those who are engaged: So that parties are, almost in the very heat of a contest, ready to listen to the dictates of humanity or reason.'[21]

Ferguson shared his optimistic illusions with some of his fellow Scottish *literati*. William Robertson, in his history characteristically entitled *The Progress of Society in Europe*, maintained that the growth of commerce unites mankind and disposes men to peace since it establishes in every state 'an order of citizens bound by their interest to be the guardians of public tranquillity.'[22] Adam Smith went further than either by envisaging man as an essentially economic animal, who reached in the fourth stage of his economic evolution the commercial state, with its elaborate social and political superstructure. The growing emphasis upon liberty and progress in terms of the acquisition of property led naturally in Britain to the Smithian discovery of *homo economicus* and the principles of laissez-faire, the encapsulation of liberty in man's self-interested determination to create an environment in which, having satisfied his basic needs, he could proceed to satisfy more complex ones.[23] By means of the overriding principle of the division of labour Smith gave to the idea of property a universal significance and to that of liberty a general recognition. But for all his insistence upon the state's role in defending the citizens, his civil government seemed to be intended primarily for the protection of the rich at the expense of the liberty of the poor. He observed in Book V of *The Wealth of Nations* that 'The acquisition of valuable and extensive property, therefore, necessarily requires the establishment of civil government . . . Civil government, so far as it is instituted for the security of property, is in reality instituted for the defence of the rich against the poor, or of those who have some property against those who have none at all.'[24]

It would be an unfair use of hindsight to criticize these men for failing to discern the fact that a new face of sovereign power, marked with the virulent sign of nationalism, was shortly to be unmasked in other parts of Europe. In the Habsburg lands of Hungary and the Austrian Netherlands nationalist revolts would destroy the ambitious plans of the Emperor Joseph II and in France after 1789 the power of nationalism would tune the engines of the Revolutionary Wars to a capacity previously undreamt of in that optimistic century. Yet it is important to note that these ideas of progress towards prosperity and liberty merely disguised the reality of state power which remained the arbiter as well as the guarantor of the citizens' liberty.

There was an exception, however, among the illustrious names of the Scottish Enlightenment, one figure who stoutly maintained that liberty depended on government and not vice-versa. The greatest mind amongst them and one of the greatest of the century, David Hume, in his *History of England* castigated John Locke and his Whig supporters for their perversity, 'forgetting that a regard to liberty, though a laudable passion, ought commonly to be subordinate to a reverence for established government.'[25]

## THE CONTRIBUTION OF THE NEW HISTORY

Reference to Hume's historical writing is a salutary reminder of the need, if we are to appreciate how the idea of progress became so influential during the eighteenth century, to turn back to that century's beginning, and away from the works of moral philosophy and political economy to those of history. For it was in the new history of the Enlightenment that man's sojourn on this planet acquired that evolutionary, anthropological perspective to which historians have generally clung. It is not to be imagined, of course, that Clio stepped, fully formed like the Botticelli Venus, out of the age of reason. For some time before the eighteenth century the antique rhetoric of the *ars historica* and the careful compilations of the *érudits* had been challenged by advocates of a new sort of history. Neither of these earlier traditions encouraged the perception of history in terms of change and development. The first concentrated on a stylized, moralizing form which sought to plunder the past to provide striking lessons for the present. The second looked on the past as a treasure-house of knowledge to be unearthed and published: ancient texts, medieval chronicles, diplomatic instructions, peace and marriage treaties, collections of laws and the records of law courts.[26]

But men like Etienne Pasquier, a French lawyer who wrote his *Recherches de la France* in 1560, were beginning to delineate a new perspective. In seeking 'a reconstruction of the past for the needs of the present', Pasquier approached some way towards the central tenet of modern historical writing, the attempt to understand how past generations developed from one another until they became the present.[27] Yet he and others like him, Jean Bodin, François

9

Baudouin, Nicolas Vignier and the Sieur de la Popelinière, were locked into a world view based on theology and jurisprudence which was not yet capable of perceiving that, in the words of Alexander Pope, 'the proper study of mankind is man'. During the seventeenth century, however, that mode of study at last became a serious one, and it was then appropriate to write the history of *homo sapiens* not only to account for man's past but also in order to understand its relationship with the present. However, to proceed in this way rather than merely to seek inspiration from past models, as in the case of dead heroes teaching later generations by their example, was to essay a revolution. In this sense most history-writing has been retrospective since the age of the Enlightenment.[28]

One of the first practitioners of this difficult art of writing history backwards was the Italian, Giambattista Vico (1668–1744), though to label him an historian is as misleading as to call his great contemporary, Johann Sebastian Bach, an organist. Vico's *Scienza Nuova* was the first attempt at producing a comprehensive study of the evolution of human society and is a work of philosophy and philology as well as of history. But his historicism is central to our theme. Vico set out to challenge the belief that past ages could be interpreted in eighteenth-century terms. At first sight, therefore, his method appears to be totally opposed to 'backward history'. In reality, however, Vico's grand design only acquired its full meaning in the light of his own world. He maintained that all societies pass through three stages which he called the divine, the heroic and the human. The last stage, governed by the dictates of fully developed human reason, reflected the growing concern with the human condition which Vico's contemporaries were beginning to exhibit. It also reflected a degree of enlightenment which implied human progress, though Vico was not especially concerned to make that point, one which would later become a political issue among eighteenth-century historians. For Vico the essence of humanity could only be trapped in man's history, which, like the lives of individual human beings, was subject to growth and maturity and ultimately to decay: inevitably since he included history as a human artefact.[29]

Vico's influence was submerged for some time after his death, until 1827. In that year the translation of *Scienza Nuova* into French by the historian, Jules Michelet, recruited the Italian's thought for the post-Kantian crusade which, as we shall see, was to define history as man's progress towards moral freedom.[30] But far more evident than Vico's work for much of the eighteenth century was the historical writing of Voltaire, which took up directly the theme of human progress viewed from the standpoint of his own age. Underlying his history *en philosophe* was the preoccupation with the human condition as man struggled against the constraints imposed by organized religion or the secular authority, or the infamous alliance of the two.

Progress towards the acquisition of liberty or regression from that coveted goal were the dominating themes of Voltaire's histories.

He began his *Siècle de Louis XIV* (1751) by announcing his intention 'to depict for posterity, not the actions of a single man, but the spirit of men in the most enlightened century that there has ever been'. That spirit was not to be discerned in the tedious elaboration of every historical event; there was much dross to be jettisoned if the pattern shaping societies, 'that which deserves the attention of all time', was to be perceived accurately. For Voltaire, chief publicist of the Enlightenment, the key was to be found in man's liberation from the stultifying forces which held him captive and hindered the full exploitation of his potential: notably, though not exclusively, organized religion. His study of the past, however, had taught him that change in this direction was tardy and not necessarily irreversible. Even that most promising development for the *philosophes*, which Voltaire called 'the enlightenment of the human spirit', worked disappointingly slowly.

> Slow in influencing the learned, reason was scarcely yet able to guide scholars, still less ordinary citizens. It must first be established in the minds of leaders, then gradually it descends and, at length, rules the people who are unaware of its existence, but who, perceiving the moderation of their superiors, learn how to imitate them. It is one of the great works of time, and the time was not yet come.[31]

Nevertheless, some seventeen years later when his *Précis du siècle de Louis XV* (1768) appeared, Voltaire was rather more optimistic about the approaching millenium. Looking back over the reign, he noted with satisfaction that an entire religious order, the Society of Jesus, had been proscribed in France by the secular power (1764) and the disciplines of other monastic orders similarly reformed; and that the secular judges headed by the *Parlement* of Paris were at odds with the episcopacy over the long-running controversy of Jansenism, surely clear indications of the progress of enlightenment and the dissipation of prejudice. He allowed himself the incautious and ill-judged observation that the eighteenth century was seeking to bring everything to perfection.[32]

Between the history of Louis XIV's reign and that of his great-grandson, Louis XV, Voltaire published in 1765 his *Philosophie de l'histoire* which he later merged into the *Essai sur les moeurs*. Although primarily concerned with aspects of the ancient world, this is plainly a work of the new history. The sociological language, à la Montesquieu, is of the nature of man and his society, and the theme, of his struggle to free himself from the blindfold of unreason, is characteristically Voltairian. He maintained that all mankind is endowed with feelings of justice and pity, and the faculty of reason

11

which 'is so constant that it subsists in spite of all the passions which fight it, in spite of tyrants who would drown it in blood, in spite of imposters who would destroy it in superstition'.[33] In the long run, Voltaire argued, that faculty would enable all people to judge whether the laws which governed them conformed to the sentiments of justice and pity which are mankind's universal birthright.

In contrast to Voltaire's cautious optimism on the subject of human progress, his compatriot, the marquis de Condorcet, embraced a linear view which was both inspiring and, in the light of his own life as well as of subsequent history, not altogether convincing. He wrote his *Esquisse d'un tableau historique des progrès de l'esprit humain* while in hiding from the Revolution which ironically he himself had welcomed, and he died in prison in 1794. It is not surprising, therefore, that his hymn to human perfectability is touched with melancholy, though not with doubt. The *Esquisse* represents in its most uncompromising form the truth received from the Enlightenment which all later generations were to inherit: that through the use of reason man could liberate himself and society from the various tyrannies which beset him. Reason and freedom were but two sides of the same coin: the single law of history decreed man's ultimate perfectability.

Condorcet identified the great obstacle in the way of this goal, an obstacle becoming more firmly lodged with each passing generation. This was so-called Machiavellism, that interpretation of political events and society which based itself upon the state's power and security rather than the subjects' liberty, upon the discrepancy between means and ends rather than their unshakeable union. He scathingly dismissed this interpretation as 'This doctrine, so dear to those who wish to act because it secures them from the empire of those who know how to think.'[34] His fears on this score, and his unwillingness to face squarely the unwelcome, insidious doctrine of machiavellism which threatened such a cynical denouement to man's progress towards perfection, were shared by Goethe's hero, Egmont, and also by the outstanding historian of the Enlightenment, Edward Gibbon. How far the 'urgent consideration of the public safety . . . may operate to dissolve the natural obligations of humanity and justice', Gibbon admitted, 'is a doctrine of which I still desire to remain ignorant': though it must be added that he did acknowledge the inevitable distancing of power from virtue in political affairs.[35]

Here we touch upon one of the major questions raised at the beginning of this book, that of whether it is possible to view the progress of political liberty other than through the distorting mirror of political realism. For it was the achievement of some powerful eighteenth-century history writing not only to reduce the doctrine of reason of state to the level of a passing prejudice, but even to persuade later generations made more cynical by abundant evidence to the contrary, that that might indeed still be the proper perception. The success of the historians of the Enlightenment depended upon their espousal of the potent idea of progress at a time when man's terrestrial situation was becoming an issue of near equal importance with that of his eternal salvation. Old loyalties were being challenged in the secular sphere as in the spiritual, and a unique opportunity for humanity to throw off the bonds of the old hierarchic world of received and unquestioned truths appeared to present itself. The methodology of the new history, written *en philosophe*, guaranteed and still guarantees that an eighteenth-century manifesto in favour of political liberty would be projected far beyond the confines of that age. Later historians would receive as a standard part of their intellectual baggage a time-capsule fashioned in the age of reason; so that an idea fathered in the eighteenth century would acquire a perennial significance in the past and present of future generations.

It is not intended in this volume to step far beyond the limits of that century save to note briefly the strongly flowing tide and one or two belated attempts to check it. Already in the 1780s one of the seminal thinkers of the Enlightenment, Immanuel Kant (1724–1804) was defining the idea of history as man's progress towards moral freedom, a progress made possible by his increasing rationality, a characteristic only capable of full development over an historic time-scale. The argument has a Lockean ring about it, though with Kant the teleological aspect is much more strongly indicated. The idealist German philosopher, G.W.F. Hegel (1770–1831) followed Kant in defining history *en philosophe* as the story of man's acquisition of liberty by the pursuit of the *idea* of liberty. Though disapproving of the overly Germanic nature of Hegel's vision, the Italian philosopher and historian, Benedetto Croce (1866–1952), recognized its potency in the hands of philosopher-historians like Victor Cousin (1792–1867) and Jules Michelet (1798–1874). He himself gave to liberty an even greater role to play in human history, as the universal moral imperative. He made it something more vital than the end-product of a long historical journey. For him it represented 'the explanatory principle of the course of history', 'the eternal creator of history and itself the subject of every history', 'the moral ideal of humanity'.[36]

A contrary view was slow to establish itself amongst historians, though perhaps the year 1931, which witnessed a two-pronged counter-attack, is a significant date and one that fits neatly into the beginning of the period of Professor Hexter's concern. In that year a remarkable essay appeared by the Cambridge historian, Herbert Butterfield, *The Whig Interpretation of History*, which continues after fifty years to proffer a formidable challenge to history *en philosophe*. His particular target was the historicist view of political liberty developing as the sturdy offspring of Protestantism, naturalized in the British parliamentary tradition; but his strictures may be levelled equally against Condorcet, Michelet or Hegel as against the British historians, Macaulay, Hallam or Acton. Butterfield was in fact re-stating the eighteenth-century opinion of the versatile German writer, J.G. von Herder (1744–1803). The latter believed that though men could only be understood in terms of their history, the societies which they form should be judged on their own terms and not according to the standard of some grand design which was no more than the passing vision of a generation falsely endowed with the aura of universality.[37] It was also in 1931 that Carl Becker delivered his Yale lectures which were subsequently published under the title of *The Heavenly City of the Eighteenth Century Philosophers*. He too attacked the philosophers' claim to speak for all generations:

> They project the conflict into the centuries so that it may be regarded as something more than an eighteenth-century squabble between Philosophers and priests, so that it may be regarded as an aspect of a conflict exemplified in all human experience, the conflict between the cosmic forces of good and evil, between the City of Light and the City of Darkness – the eternal conflict for the soul of man.[38]

Since 1931 history has been given many shapes, though Butterfield's emphasis upon contingency and 'the analysis of all the mediations by which the past was turned into our present' prefigures the quasi-existentialism of some recent scholarship.[39] But if professional historians have had increasing doubts about whether to depict the past as a progressively civilizing and liberating odyssey, that has not been the case in the public at large. Nor should we be surprised that man, subjected to the lowering pressures of the cataclysmic events of the last two centuries, has chosen to cling fast to the eighteenth century's golden thread of individual liberty. Since that age of reason not only the totalitarian regimes of Left and Right, but even the moderate democracies of the Centre have steadily increased their demands on their citizens' loyalty. The separation of private morality from the imperative of public safety has become total. The argument in favour of state authority as the guarantor of individual political liberty has been demonstrably undermined. One might go further: the unfettered freedom of action which must now be allowed to the state in the interests of security is as much challenged as it is justified by the honourable ideal of political liberty. Against this background it has been far too easy for politicians and publicists to exploit the situation. Indeed, opinion-formers in general have taken the initiative in deploying all the arguments, in Butterfield's phrase, 'that are so handy to men when discussion is dragged into the market place and philosophy is dethroned by common sense; so that it is no simple matter to demonstrate how the whig historian, from his mountain-top, sees the course of history only inverted and aslant'.[40]

# REFERENCES AND NOTES

1. Quentin Skinner, *The Foundations of Modern Political Thought*, 2 vols (Cambridge 1978), I, pp. 117–28.
2. Howell A. Lloyd, *The State, France and the Sixteenth Century* (London 1983), p. 159.
3. J. Bodin, *The Six Books of a Commonweal*, trans. Richard Knolles and ed. K. D. McRae (Cambridge, Mass. 1962), Book I, Ch. 6, pp. 46– 7, 69.
4. D. Parker, 'Law, society and the state in the thought of Jean Bodin', *History of Political Thought*, II, 2 (1981), p. 284.
5. Lloyd, *op. cit.*, p. 112.
6. F. A. Mann, 'Outlines of a history of expropriation', *The Law Quarterly Review*, vol. 75 (1959), pp. 194–6, 202–3.
7. Theodore K. Rabb, *The Struggle for Stability in Early Modern Europe* (Oxford 1975), *op cit.*, p. 72.
8. Note Spinoza's view expressed in the *Tractatus Theologico-Politicus* (1670), that kings ruled by a kind of confidence trick based upon their subjects' religious fears. P. Hazard, *La crise de la conscience européene*, 3 vols (Paris 1935), vol. I, p. 185.
9. *Discours de la méthode*, in *Oeuvres de Descartes*, new edn, C. Adam and P. Tannery (Paris 1965), vol. 6, pp. 1–2. R. J. White, *The Anti-Philosophers* (London 1970), p. 18.
10. *Méditations*, in *Oeuvres de Descartes*, new edn, C. Adam and P. Tannery (Paris 1964), vol. 9, Pt I, p. 22.
11. Thomas Hobbes, *Leviathan*, Scolar Press Facsimile of the London 1651 edn, (Menston 1969), p. 93.
12. *Ibid.*, pp. 110–11, 114.
13. John Locke, *Two Treatises of Government*, ed. P. Laslett (Cambridge 1960), pp. 326–7.
14. C. B. Macpherson, *The Political Theory of Possessive Individualism: Hobbes to Locke* (Oxford 1962). Note too W. van Leyden's more recent analysis of the work of the two philosophers: *Hobbes and Locke: the Politics of Freedom and Obligation* (London 1981).
15. G. S. Holmes, *Augustan England. Professions, State and Society, 1680– 1730* (London 1982), p. 239. See also J. H. Plumb, *The Growth of Political Stability in England, 1675–1725* (London, 1967), pp. 114–23.
16. P. B. Munsche, *Gentlemen and Poachers: The English game laws 1671– 1831* (Cambridge 1981), p. 127.
17. E. P. Thompson, 'The moral economy of the English crowd in the eighteenth century', *Past and Present*, 50 (1971), 122–6.
18. Adam Ferguson, *Essay on the History of Civil Society*, ed. Duncan Forbes (Edinburgh 1966), Part IV, Section III, p. 189.
19. Adam Ferguson, *Principles of Moral and Political Science*, 2 vols (Hildersheim 1975), vol. 1, pp. 461–3.
20. *Ibid.*, p. 512.
21. *Ibid.*, p. 295.
22. William Robertson, *The Progress of Society in Europe*, ed. F. Gilbert (Chicago 1972), p. 67.

23. A. S. Skinner, 'Adam Smith: an economic interpretation of history', in *Essays on Adam Smith*, ed. A. S. Skinner and T. Wilson (Oxford 1975), p. 174.

24. Adam Smith, *An Enquiry into the Nature and Causes of the Wealth of Nations*, ed. R. H. Campbell and A. S. Skinner, 2 vols (Oxford 1976), pp. 710, 715. See also the comments by Duncan Forbes, 'Sceptical Whiggism, commerce and liberty', *Essays on Adam Smith*, ed. Skinner and Wilson (Oxford 1975), p. 184.

25. David Hume, *History of England*, 8 vols (Oxford 1826), vol. 8, p. 284.

26. O. Ranum, *Artisans of Glory: Writers and historical thought in seventeenth-century France* (North Carolina 1980), pp. 17 ff. D. R. Kelley, *Foundations of Modern Historical Scholarship* (New York 1970), pp. 129–41, 215 ff.

27. G. Huppert, *The Idea of Perfect History: Historical erudition and historical philosophy in Renaissance France* (Illinois 1969), p. 34.

28. For a characteristically stimulating essay on this subject see Hugh Trevor-Roper, 'The historical philosophy of the enlightenment', in *Studies on Voltaire and the Eighteenth Century*, XXVII (1963), 1667–87.

29. B. A. Haddock, *An Introduction to Historical Thought* (London 1980), p. 62. T. G. Bergin and M. H. Fisch have translated *The New Science*, providing a particularly cogent version in their abridged edition (New York 1961). See in particular paragraphs 245, 247–9, 331–2, 393, 1096. Vico's view of history is discussed by A. R. Caponigri, *Time and Idea. The Theory of History in Giambattista Vico* (London 1953); and by L. Pompa, *Vico, a Study of the New Science* (Cambridge 1975).

30. J. B. Bury, *The Idea of Progress* (London 1928), pp. 267–71.

31. Voltaire, François Marie Arouet, *Le Siècle de Louis XIV* in *Oeuvres Historiques*, ed. R. Pomeau (Paris 1957), pp. 616, 620, 1063.

32. Voltaire, *Précis du siècle de Louis XV* in *Oeuvres Historiques*, ed. R. Pomeau (Paris 1957), pp. 1566–71.

33. Voltaire, *La philosophie de l'histoire*, ed. J. H. Brumfitt (Geneva 1969), Ch. 7, p. 114.

34. Quoted by K. M. Baker, *Condorcet* (Chicago 1975), p. 347. For the *Esquisse* itself, I have used the text edited by M. and F. Hincker (Paris 1966), which reprints the original version housed in the Bibliothèque de l'Institut de France in Paris.

35. L. Gossmann, *The Empire Unpossess'd: an essay on Gibbon's 'Decline and Fall'* (Cambridge 1981), pp. 49 ff. See too the article by A. Momigliano, 'Gibbon's contribution to historical method', *Historia*, vol. 2 (1954), pp. 450–63. In his optimistic coda to Chapter 38 of *The Decline and Fall of the Roman Empire*, ed. J. B. Bury, 7 vols (London 1909–14), IV, 180, Edward Gibbon remarks that 'we cannot determine to what height the human species may aspire in their advances towards perfection; but it may safely be presumed that no people, unless the face of nature is changed, will relapse into their original barbarism'. Much depends, of course, upon the definition of barbarism; in which context cf. the observations of A. B. Cobban, *In Search of Humanity* (London 1960), p. 242, where he writes of 'the increasing re-brutalization of contemporary life'. Cobban's thought-provoking work deserves close study.

36. Bury, *op.cit.*, pp. 243–56. B. Croce, *History as the Story of Liberty* (London 1941), p. 59. For further comment on the role of history in the German Enlightenment, see below pp. 118–19.
37. Isaiah Berlin, *Vico and Herder* (London 1976), p. 198.
38. Carl L. Becker, *The Heavenly City of the Eighteenth Century Philosophers* (Yale 1960 edn.) pp. 105–6.
39. H. Butterfield, *The Whig Interpretation of History* (London 1931), p.47.
40. *Ibid.*, p. 14.

# Chapter two

# FRANCE (I): CROWN AND NOBILITY

## FRANCE AND ENGLAND COMPARED

In France the concept of the ultimate impersonal authority of the state was slow to emerge. That was because legitimate kingship retained its highly personal hold on the body politic, a fact which in turn prevented the subjects from enjoying anything approaching equal status in the eyes of the monarch. The key to an understanding of the French political order was to be found in the relationship between the crown and the nobility. Even as late as the eighteenth century only some one per cent of the French population were nobles, yet they owned between a quarter and a third of the land. Their privileges were considerable, including exemption from the *taille*, the chief direct tax of *ancien régime* France. In many ways they may be compared with the English gentry, whose social and economic status similarly enabled them to corner the highest offices in the church, the army and the navy, and whose local function as justices of the peace matched the wide-ranging judicial powers of the French *seigneurs*.[1]

The English gentry did differ in two crucial respects, however, from the French *noblesse*. First, legally speaking they were indistinguishable from the rest of the population, whereas membership of the second estate made the French nobility into a distinctive group. The latter did not carry the tax burdens of other social groups. They could claim special rights at law denied to non-nobles and a range of symbolic, honorific privileges intended simply to underline their separate corporate identity: the right to wear silk and carry swords, to sport crests over their coats-of-arms and mount gallows at the entrance to their *châteaux*. In addition, their ownership of property was of a kind denied to non-noble owners in their *seigneurie*. Whereas in England full private ownership, especially of land, had long been an established principle, in France a variety of feudal privileges further differentiated the *seigneur* from every other group of the king's subjects: the right to collect an annual fee from all tenants of the *seigneurie* and another for permission to sell land: the right to claim a percentage of the produce of all the land in the lordship and to require its inhabitants to use the *seigneur*'s oven, mill or wine-press.[2]

The second crucial difference between the English gentry and the French nobility was to be found in their relationship with government. From the turn of the eighteenth century, the period of the Revolution Settlement, the principle of legal equality of citizens had cleared the way in England for the emergence of the concept of the impersonal state, disinterestedly demanding and receiving the loyalty of all the subjects. True that power more often than not assumed the visage of the men of property who were its most conspicuous servants. Yet they too were bound by the same law, and on the whole they found it advantageous to be so.[3] In matters of taxation that sense of equal, universal involvement in the political nation was reflected in the belief that everyone was obliged to share the burden because all profited by the protection thus afforded to life and liberty. However, a parallel view also existed, that poor people should be exempted from taxation if at all possible because of the hardship that even moderate taxes might inflict on them. Walpole's re-imposition of the salt tax in 1732 brought the two views into conflict, for nobody would be able to avoid paying the salt tax though many would suffer great hardship in the paying. A characteristically British compromise promised to resolve the dilemma by the end of the century. Taxes on luxuries rather than on necessities did not exempt the poor on principle, but they left them free to avoid taxation if they chose.[4] The point about the English attitude is that it reflected no sense of government obligation to bestow privileges upon one part of the citizenry at the expense of others. Behind the facade of king, lords and commons, and the related local infrastructure of squires and justices of the peace, lurked an authority which guarded the interests and therefore held the loyalty of all. Such a power, by the very nature of its universality, transcended the personal and therefore had no need to purchase loyalty.

In France the situation was quite different. The Crown was still strongly identified with the head of the ruling house, a person as much as an institution. The monarch remained preoccupied with groups rather than with individuals and chiefly with that group, the nobility, whose relationship with the king was central to French politics for much of the *ancien régime*. During the critical years of the late sixteenth century, when France was racked by the civil Wars of Religion it had seemed fleetingly possible that the ruling alliance of throne and nobility might be overthrown. For three years (1588–91) the Committee of the Sixteen held sway in Paris. This group of Catholic fanatics opposed the king, Henry III, and drove him from his capital. They also included in their ranks social climbers, who were willing to take extreme measures to satisfy their own ambitions. Eventually their ruthless, terrorizing regime, which prefigured the notorious French Revolutionary Committee of Public Safety, frightened their erstwhile noble allies. At the close of 1591 the leading members of the Sixteen were either executed or imprisoned by the Duc de Mayenne, a member of the leading Catholic family of Guise.[5] Some eighteen months later Henry of Navarre's abjuration of Protestantism gave him undisputed recognition as king by re-uniting him to the Catholic majority. This event signalled the end of the Religious Wars.

The restoration of royal authority under Henry IV also restored the nobility to its accustomed place in the sun. It is true that first Richelieu and then Louis XIV tried to change the nature of the nobility's political relationship with the Crown, a subject discussed below, but neither desired to rule other than through that order. The Princes of the Blood and some of the old ruling families may have been dismissed from the council chamber, but their replacements, families like the Bouthillier, Phélypeaux and Colbert, were within a generation or two represented by a glittering array of marquises and counts. It was a similar story with the intendants, the government's chief representatives in the provinces during the last century and a half of the old order. Already in the 1630s, intendants' families formed the top one per cent of Parisian society, most of them well-established in the *robe* nobility. In the eighteenth century too, it was most unusual to find intendants who were only first-generation noblemen.[6] Indeed, historians have traditionally asserted that in the closing decades of the *ancien régime* the nobility tried to tighten its hold upon the country's social and political life. This belief in a so-called 'aristocratic reaction', characterized by attempts to revive archaic seigneurial dues and to deprive non-nobles of opportunities for advancement, has recently been challenged.[7] Yet there is no doubt that both Louis XV and his successor continued to rely on the traditional recruiting grounds of the court and high administrative nobility.

## THE 'CONTRACT' UNDER PRESSURE

The essential mechanism supporting the regime, which was the contract between king and nobility, survived down to the Revolution. But we shall see that it did so under increasing stress as the government's demands threatened to overrun its ally's ground. The pressure was unremitting though the objectives were usually short-term and the implications rarely perceived. Having emerged relatively victorious from the crisis of authority which had beset France during the sixteenth-century Wars of Religion, the Bourbon monarchy was bound to raise its sights in order to assert the new authority which victory had brought. It was necessary, too, for French kings to take measures to neutralize those pressures, both within and beyond French frontiers, which had precipitated the crisis in the first place. They had to overcome the resentment of men who were being displaced by new officials from what they believed to be their rightful position as the king's closest advisers. They had to raise the revenues necessary to arm France adequately against her enemies, an operation beyond the royal means if traditional limits on the king's right to levy taxes were to be observed. Yet the Habsburgs' pincer threat to France's frontiers posed a challenge to security which the king was obliged to meet.

Gradually within the framework of the ancient polity the Crown began to chisel out a new structure of relationships. The notion of kingship, of royal sovereignty in France, contained two potentially contradictory elements, those of office and property.[8] Part of the French tradition emphasized the king's role as executor of the kingdom rather than as owner of the crown: another aspect underlined his right to inherit, by an absolute and fundamental law, the throne and land of France. Both themes were discernible in the attitudes of Henry IV. However, his overriding need to establish the legitimacy of his cause after the religious and political tergiversations of the civil war years led Henry increasingly to emphasize the proprietorial authority that flowed to him via his right of succession. A measure of the king's predilection for the proprietorial element was the frequent use in his correspondence of the possessive adjective: '*my* cities', '*my* state'.

At this time, too close an identification of the Crown with the concept of office risked resurrecting the idea of the king as merely the administrator of the realm. This idea had been well aired by Huguenot writers of the 1570s, men like François Hotman and the authors of the *Vindiciae contra Tyrannos*. They preached that the king was no more than the people's nominee. As Bodin caustically observed in the same decade, such a relationship made the exercise of royal power a matter of sufferance rather than sovereignty.[9] With the firm re-establishment of royal authority, however, the advantages to be gained by central government from emphasizing this alternative idea of kingly office became apparent. The obligation of administering rather than merely possessing the kingdom implied a more active, positive, even interventionist role for the crown than hitherto. It was important though, in the interests of firm government, that the administrative attribute of kingship should be detached from any sense of responsibility to the people. An alternative source of royal accountability would ultimately present itself, in the shadowy form of the impersonal state.

However, any moves in that direction would have grave implications for the nobility whose relationship with the king provided the hinge that ensured the effective working of the political order. Yet Louis XIII's principal minister, Cardinal Richelieu, believed that it was necessary to harness noble energies more directly to the state's needs. Thus he greatly expanded the definition of *lèse-majesté*, itself a highly personalized concept of treason, to include noble support for any member of the royal family involved in factious opposition to government policies, the writing or publishing of seditious libels, even military negligence. Although the Cardinal was committed to the maintenance of the privileged noble order, he was adamant that it must accept what a later commentator has called an 'unmitigated subservience to the state'.[10] This subservience was reinforced in the early part of Louis XIV's reign as the definition of nobility itself came under scrutiny. Louis's chief mentor, Cardinal Mazarin, had urged the young king to preserve the privileges of the nobility and this he did, though not without a further tightening of the screw of central government control vis-à-vis its traditional ally. The intendants in the provinces were ordered by Colbert in 1667 to investigate titles of nobility. As a result, proof of noble status shifted from the private domain of particular families' claims and reputation, to a legal, government-approved document, the *ordonnance de maintenir de noblesse*. The second estate was being effectively penned by the servants of a more *dirigiste* monarchy. Colbert's enquiries also had the effect of narrowing the distinction between *noblesse de robe* and *noblesse d'épée*, a fact which draws attention to the significance of venality in France, and in particular its importance in modifying the relationship between Crown and nobility.[11]

The concept of venality or sale of office precisely reflected the twin notions which underlay the concept of French kingship itself, the proprietorial and the administrative, a fact which seriously inhibited the emergence of the idea of the state in eighteenth-century France.[12] The Crown's practice of selling financial or judicial offices, many of them conferring hereditary nobility either immediately or in the third generation, had its origins around the turn of the fifteenth-sixteenth centuries. With the institution of the *paulette* in 1604, an annual tax clearing the way for the transmission of office within families, venality became a firmly established feature of the king's government. One result of this fact was that the working partnership between crown and nobility was able to survive, despite the former's growing demands upon the latter. Indeed, it prospered to the extent that the new office-holding nobility possessed the education and professional training necessary to run an increasingly complex administration. Most of the ministers and intendants appointed under Richelieu, Mazarin and Louis XIV came from such families. In time, however, that working relationship would become a barrier to necessary reform and then venality would help to prevent it from being dismantled. The opposition of independent, institutional office-holders, notably members of the sovereign courts, to government initiatives that threatened to overturn traditional policies, was a prominent feature of the declining years of the *ancien régime*.

More generally it was obviously the case that office, viewed as personal property as well as an administrative function, like any other sort of personal possession, would be employed in the best interests of the owner. These private interests would not necessarily coincide with the public obligations attached to it. Already in the sixteenth century arguments against the sale of judicial offices in particular had regularly been advanced. However, this criticism was in vain, for such sales brought in much-needed financial revenues which, though by no means adequate in wartime, were less difficult to collect than traditional taxes.[13] But the long-term price for such financial topping-up was the Crown's acceptance of a regime administered by officials whose loyalty was not to a disembodied state employing them on a salaried basis; instead it was to the king, the guarantor of their property. Venality, in other words, emphasized the personal bond between the Crown and its chief agents. Impersonality implies equality of treatment, and conversely it may be correctly inferred that such personal links reinforced the traditional inequalities within the French kingdom, held in place by the key relationship between the Crown and the second estate. As Louis XIV began his majority, liberty under the Bourbon kings still consisted in the maintenance of the various rights and privileges enjoyed by each of the separate orders of the kingdom.

## LOUIS XIV, PROPRIETARY MONARCH

With his pride in the Bourbon dynasty and his determination to rule his country in person, Louis XIV was temperamentally well-equipped to emphasize the proprietorial aspect of his kingship. He believed that he represented a line of 'hereditary kings, who can boast that there isn't either a better house, nor greater power, nor more absolute authority than theirs anywhere else in the world'. He explained to his son his decision to take effective control after Mazarin's death in 1661 in characteristically patrimonial language: 'I began, therefore, to cast my eyes over all the various parts of the state, and not casual eyes, but the eyes of a master, deeply struck at not finding a single one that did not cry out for my attention.'[14] He prided himself upon this personal initiative which was to be apotheosized in Charles Le Brun's great painting, entitled *le roi gouverne par lui-même*, on the ceiling of the Hall of Mirrors in Versailles.

The palace itself provides further evidence of the king's proprietorial image. Versailles was at once the centre of government and the ruler's country residence. The council room where critical decisions affecting the whole of Europe were taken was literally next door to the royal bedchamber. That most private of rooms was symbolically located – after the architect Hardouin-Mansart's late seventeenth-century reconstruction – at the very heart of the *château*. Those advisers who assisted the king in his *conseil d'en haut* held the title of minister not ex-officio but only because, and so long as, the king chose to summon them. The king's guests, nobles bearing some of the most distinguished names in France, made up a perennial house-party, flattered to be invited, anxious to be noticed, eager to please. Even the raising of extraordinary revenue for war had its proprietorial dimension at Versailles. Not for the Bourbons the banking techniques of their maritime rivals, the English and the Dutch, but a dismantling and melting down of the family silver, tables, balustrades, candlesticks and chandeliers from the Hall of Mirrors and the *Salon* of Mercury.

Such an unsophisticated method of raising funds, like the practice of selling offices, was evidence of the abiding power of French dynasticism, but also of its relative weakness when compared with its formidable rival across the Channel. For a philosophy of government based on personality and exclusivity limited the subjects' obligations far more drastically than one based on an impersonal, universal legislator. In international terms, therefore, the power of Louis XIV's France shrank dramatically when compared with England's resources. In Wallerstein's aphoristic comment, 'The rhetoric of strength (*L'Etat, c'est moi*) is frequently a substitute for the reality.'[15]

And what of the rhetoric of tyranny versus liberty, by which some contemporary commentators identified the struggle between Louis XIV and his English enemy? The English, Voltaire tells us in his *Lettres philosophiques*, 'are not only jealous of their own liberty but jealous too to preserve the liberty of others. The English were bent on pursuing Louis XIV solely because of his ambition. They made war against him willingly with no other interest in mind.'[16] Voltaire was of course naively repeating views imbibed on his English visit in the 1720s, but views nevertheless which faithfully reflected this well-known antithesis between liberty and tyranny. The tyranny of which Louis stood accused appeared to consist of two components: the exercise of his personal power when viewed against the complementary inequality of his subjects' rights; and his military enterprises which, had they been successful, might have led to the revival of absolutist governments in England and the United Provinces. The second factor also carried the implication of an intolerant crusade to be launched by Louis after his expulsion of the Huguenots from France in 1685. To the Protestant powers this act appeared to be the preliminary to further aggression.[17] This was a view to which

Voltaire was happy to subscribe. Yet he was distinctly partial in his interpretation of each country's security needs. It is true that dynastic kings and military men were old comrades-in-arms but security was an old problem too, though one which an island power had to tackle by other than military means. England's successful naval wars against the Dutch in the early part of Louis XIV's reign, the favourable terms which she obtained at the peace of Utrecht in 1713, and later her eighteenth-century triumph in the colonial struggle in America, indicated her equal preoccupation with security. Voltaire knew this perfectly well, and in his chapter on commerce in the *Lettres philosophiques* observed how trade had enabled the English to establish their navy and thereby acquire the mastery of the seas. Yet he chose to emphasize the liberty bestowed upon the English by commerce rather than the measures taken to secure it.[18] The contrast between his own country's military ethos and England's trading spirit explains his preference, though only when we recall that Voltaire had his own point to make, that absolutism did not pay.

Voltaire's letters on the English suggest an under-estimation of the capacity of the British parliamentary state to coerce all its subjects, and an over-estimation of the French king's ability to do the same. Indeed, questions which were potentially destructive of royal authority were already being asked in France, implying a division between the king's interests and those of his people. Archbishop Fénelon, tutor to the king's eldest grandson, the Duke of Burgundy, was obliquely addressing Louis XIV himself when he asked the prince, 'Have you carefully examined whether your people needed war in which you have become involved? It may only have concerned some claim to a succession affecting you personally; your people may have had no real interest in it. What does it matter to them if you acquire another province'; and again, accusingly, 'Have you never regarded your personal glory as a reason for undertaking some project, for fear of passing your life without distinguishing yourself from other princes?'[19] Such rhetorical questions were given greater force by reference to the king's own memoirs where, under the year 1667 and with a degree of nonchalance, Louis had noted that 'Kings, who are born to possess everything and to command over everything, must not be ashamed to accede to renown.'[20]

## LOUIS XIV, ADMINISTRATIVE MONARCH

Yet even during the reign of Louis XIV there is to be glimpsed upon closer inspection an alternative view, for the concept of the king's office, of kingship exercised as an administrative function, continued to evolve. The *métier du roi* – the craft of kingship – was Louis' own phrase, suggesting the need for a skilled professional to govern, not an amateur content to have been born, in the words of Lord Acton, upon the steps of the throne.[21] For all its personal direction and control by the monarch, his conciliar system was gradually becoming more professional, specialized and institutionalized. Symptomatic of changing times too was the diminishing role of the chancellor, the king's chief judicial officer, in matters of government. From the time of the great Colbert his place was increasingly taken over by administrators, the secretaries of state and the controller-general of finance, whose functions threatened to superimpose upon the royal image of justiciar that of *le roi bureaucrate*.[22]

If we draw back our focus from the royal bedchamber at Versailles to take in a more panoramic view of the palace, we will at once observe the new ministerial wing, built to house the government's records and the increasingly influential *bureaux* whose officials translated the results of conciliar discussion into formal policy statements. A few miles away in the Louvre a further *dépôt* for older archival materials was established. There, too, Colbert's nephew, the marquis de Torcy, who was Louis XIV's last secretary of state for foreign affairs and the most influential minister in the king's declining years, set up his political academy for the training of career diplomats. Already the secretary of state had persuaded the king to provide government money for the salaries of secretaries employed by diplomats, an expense previously borne by the diplomats themselves. Indeed the area of foreign affairs provides strong evidence of incipient bureaucratization. It has been estimated that in the last years of the reign twenty coaches were required to transport Torcy's staff of secretaries, interpreters, archivists, code clerks, heads of *bureaux* and the rest.[23]

Nor was the king's own attitude to foreign affairs always as dynastically centred as critics like Fénelon alleged. The War of Devolution against Spain in 1667–68 was a case in point. This conflict apparently turned on the jurists' interpretation of the law of succession in Brabant. On behalf of his queen, Maria Theresa, Louis and his lawyers claimed that the rights of the daughter of the late king of Spain, Philip IV, by his first marriage could not be superseded by the claims of a son born of a second marriage. On the basis of this private Brabantine law, Louis demanded large areas of the Spanish Netherlands including Luxembourg, Artois and Upper Guelderland. In fact a glance at the map indicates how the acquisition of these territories would help to counter Paris's proximity and vulnerability to a hostile Spanish Netherlands, a threat of which Louis was uneasily aware.

The Spanish partition treaties of 1698 and 1700, negotiated with the arch-enemy, William III of England, provide another example of Louis' departure from pure dynasticism. They represent a tentative move towards the principle of collective security. This was at the expense of support for the idea of the inalienability of patrimonial or (to use the contemporary legal phrase) entailed estates. As the death of Charles II, the childless king of Spain, approached, Louis faced a dilemma. He believed that the hereditary claim of his son the Dauphin acquired through Louis' queen, the Infanta Maria Theresa, was superior to all rival claims. However, the cost of implementing that hereditary claim against European-wide opposition would be incalculable. Louis preferred therefore to negotiate a division of the vast European and overseas Empire of Spain between the various candidates for the succession. What was particularly significant about this decision was his choice of ally. William III himself had no claim to the Spanish succession but he wielded great power and influence in Europe. Louis sought his assistance in the belief that together they could impose a settlement which, though it would reduce the French royal family's share of the inheritance, would prevent the outbreak of a potentially devastating war on the continent and overseas.[24]

Although the language of international affairs tended throughout Louis XIV's reign to remain that of the civil lawyer, reflecting there-fore in the public domain the rules governing private possession, the overriding requirements of security usually dictated the outcome. Such subtle shifts in emphasis from proprietorial towards administrative kingship are far more readily discernible to historians than they were to contemporaries. Down to the end of Louis XIV's reign there seemed little likelihood in the short term of a breakdown in the all-important relationship between the Crown and the privileged property-owners. The durability of this alliance was due in general terms to the innate social conservatism of both partners, and in particular to those two aspects of royal authority which together sanctioned the validity of the *status quo*, the king's judicial role and his relationship with the Almighty.

## THE CHIEF JUSTICIAR

The law, some kind of law, must of course play a central role in every political organization, and a special case has to be made if the judicial role of the French ruler is to be singled out as being of particular significance. Across the Channel in England the political process had developed around Parliament, and in the eighteenth century as in the twentieth, a proportion of members of the House of Commons was still drawn from the legal profession. As Sir Lewis Namier drily remarked, 'The connection between the courts of law and the High Court of Parliament is so obvious that it is hardly necessary to enlarge upon it.' However, the number of lawyers in the Commons was not high as a proportion of the total membership. There were six general elections in the period between 1754 and 1790, in each of which a total of 558 members were elected; only about 160 lawyers served as members of Parliament during this time.[25] The French *Parlement* of Paris was in some respects analagous to the English Parliament. It was the highest court of appeal in the land where the king's justice was dispensed and to which on great state occasions and at moments of legal or constitutional crisis, the king himself came to preside at his *lit de justice*. It also maintained as a natural concomitant of its judicial function a political tradition dating back to the fourteenth century. Then the practice was established of drawing up critical remonstrances against royal legislative acts of which the court disapproved. In the eighteenth century the *Parlement* of Paris, made up of some 230 magistrates, held on to its political influence, though not always in a fashion acceptable to the Crown. But not only were these institutional counsellors lawyers, so were the majority of the king's advisers. Of some 125 members of the royal council in the eighteenth century, the chancellors, the controllers-general of finance (with the single exception of the Scotsman, John Law), a majority of the secretaries of state, all but six of the thirty counsellors of state (most of whom had come through the ranks of the *maîtres des requêtes*, high-ranking magistrates whose office had originally denoted service in the royal household) and of course all eighty *maîtres des requêtes* themselves, had a legal background. The highest rank of provincial administration was likewise lawyer-dominated: 'The overwhelming number of intendants during the eighteenth century had been sovereign-court magistrates before entering the royal service.'[26]

How are we to account for a judicial ethos so powerful that it was not even considered untoward for Louis XIV to pronounce judicial verdicts on issues of foreign policy?[27] The answer is to be found in the king's legitimacy as ruler by virtue of a law of succession unbroken since the coming of the Capetian dynasty in 987. At first custom had dictated the succession, but after the exclusion of the daughter of Louis X in favour of the king's brother, Philip V, in 1316, and the failure of Edward III of England to maintain his claim through his mother against the first Valois king, Philip VI, the fundamental law of succession was established.[28] It survived the assassination of kings (both Henry III and Henry IV were followed by their legitimate successors), changes in political theory which threatened it obliquely,[29] and direct legislative attacks against it. The Edict of Union (1588) sought to exclude the rightful heir to the throne, Henry of Navarre, on the grounds of his Protestantism; while in 1714 Louis XIV declared his bastard sons, The Duc du Maine and the Comte de Toulouse, legitimate princes of the blood and capable of succeeding to the throne of France. Neither of these acts succeeded. The first failed to prevent Henry IV's accession while still a Protestant, and the second was annulled in 1717 by an edict recalling the fact that kings were not free thus to tamper with the fundamental law.[30] It was fortunate for the peace of Europe that the renunciation of his rights to the French throne extracted from King Philip V of Spain at the peace of Utrecht, was not put to the test, for neither he nor his successors believed that those rights had been lost.

The king of France, therefore, was bound by the fundamental law of his succession which could be neither amended nor ignored. Whereas in Britain Parliament could change the constitution as readily as it could legislate on anything else, in France the law of succession was fixed, and beyond the power of government to alter. The effect of this kingship by legal summons was to concentrate political authority in the person of the man thus summoned and to inhibit the growth of the idea of power exercised on behalf of an impersonal state. In England there was no such continuity in the history of kingship. During the period stretching from Hugh Capet's accession in 987 to the execution of Louis XVI in 1793, the English royal succession suffered innumerable fractures which ultimately diminished the king's personal authority and rendered it vulnerable to parliamentary control. William the Conqueror usurped the throne in 1066, Stephen in the following century and Henry IV at the turn of the fifteenth. The Wars of the Roses followed, with the murders of Henry VI and Edward V until finally the usurpation of Henry Tudor brought the civil strife to an end. In the seventeenth century Charles I's execution was followed during the Interregnum by an alternative political order, before his heir's eventual restoration. The exclusion shortly afterwards of James II and his Stuart descendants, to be replaced first by a Dutchman and later by a line of Hanoverian electors, was testimony to the triumph of the flexible instrument of parliamentary statute over the rigid rules of hereditary, legal and divine right monarchy. By the same token the growing power of the common law in England weakened the monarchy in comparison with France where fundamental law was reinforced by an unbroken succession.

## GOD'S LIEUTENANT

The king of France's role as God's lieutenant in his kingdom, *le roi très chrétien*, was the second powerful influence in favour of the *status quo*. Its most significant effect was to reinforce the unquestioning validation of the established order. The idea of God's lieutenancy as a sanction for the ruler's authority was deeply embedded in the French absolutist tradition, though from the beginning of the seventeenth century it was more powerfully enunciated.[31] It did not offer *carte blanche* for royal actions but support for that tradition of legally limited authority which was the Crown's great strength. The idea of divine right had another advantage. It inhibited too close an examination and analysis of the fountain head of royal government. The 'mystery of the monarchy' enabled the king, guided by the Almighty, to sense and interpret his country's needs and to act in its interests, even though others might not appreciate the virtues of his actions. In the words of Joseph Klaits, 'Divine-right monarchy, in both theory and practice under Louis XIV, was constructed upon principles which explicitly eliminated sovereignty from the realm of the rational and consigned it instead to the shadowy world of authority and tradition.'[32]

But as the power of the Divine Right idea began to weaken, a more dispassionate scrutiny of the nature of royal authority became possible. Professor Klaits suggests a portent of this development. He sees the political academy established by Torcy in 1713 as a valiant if prematurely aborted experiment in rational politics.[33] The likely effect of analysing a governmental structure so inhibited by legal constraints would be to boost the administrative at the expense of the proprietorial concept of kingship. In addition it would bring into sharper focus the special relationship between Crown and nobility and impose an increasing strain upon it. No sooner had Divine Right kingship suffered the grievous blow of Louis XIV's death than precisely this kind of analysis was applied, and by an influential figure who, albeit briefly, held the key post of controller-general of finance during the minority of Louis XV. This was the Scottish economic theorist, John Law.

## REFERENCES AND NOTES

1. See the comments of Immanuel Wallerstein, *The Modern World System*, vol. II: *Mercantilism and the Consolidation of the European World Economy, 1600–1750* (London 1980), p. 285.
2. Roland E. Mousnier, *The Institutions of France under the Absolute Monarchy, 1598–1789*, vol. 1: *Society and the State* (London 1979), pp. 112 ff. provides an authoritative survey of the rights of the noble order. See too the volume by Michael Bush, *Noble Privilege* (Manchester 1983), *passim*. On the distinctive nature of English landowning, see Alan Macfarlane, *The Origins of English Individualism* (Oxford 1978), especially Chapter 7.
3. Note the comments of E. P. Thompson, *Whigs and Hunters* (London 1975), p. 265.
4. William Kennedy, *English Taxation, 1640–1799* (London 1964), pp. 99 ff.
5. Mark Greengrass, *France in the Age of Henry IV* (London 1984), pp. 41 ff. Two stimulating articles deal with the subject of the Sixteen: J. H. M. Salmon, 'The Paris Sixteen, 1584–94: the social analysis of a revolutionary movement', *Journal of Modern History*, 44 (1972), 540–73; and H. G. Koenigsberger, 'The organisation of revolutionary

parties in France and the Netherlands during the sixteenth century', *Journal of Modern History*, 27 (1955), 349–51.

6. Richard Bonney, *Political Change in France under Richelieu and Mazarin, 1624–1661* (Oxford 1978), p. 87. Vivian R. Gruder, *The Royal Provincial Intendants: A Governing Elite in Eighteenth-Century France* (Ithaca 1968), 139.

7. Notably by William Doyle, 'Was there an aristocratic reaction in pre-revolutionary France?' *Past and Present*, 57 (1972), 97–122.

8. Herbert H. Rowen, *The King's State: Proprietary Dynasticism in Early Modern France* (New Brunswick 1980), deals extensively with this dichotomy. The author's debt to Professor Rowen's work at this stage of the argument is evident from succeeding footnote references.

9. Rowen, *op. cit.*, pp. 38–41.

10. William F. Church, *Richelieu and Reason of State* (Princeton 1972), pp. 176, 179, 185–6. See too J. H. Elliott, *Richelieu and Olivares* (Cambridge 1984), p. 136, and Nannerl O. Keohane, *Philosophy and the State in France* (Princeton 1980), p. 178.

11. Bonney, *op. cit.*, pp. 436–8.

12. Rowen, *op. cit.*, pp. 55–6.

13. Howell A. Lloyd, *The State, France and the Sixteenth Century* (London 1983), p. 73; Rowen, *op. cit.*, p. 55.

14. *Louis XIV: Mémoires for the Instruction of the Dauphin*, ed. P. Sonnino (New York 1970), p. 24.

15. Wallerstein, *op. cit.*, II, p. 114.

16. Voltaire, François Marie Arouet, *Lettres philosophiques*, ed. G. Lanson, 2 vols (Paris 1924), I, p. 90.

17. R. M. Hatton, 'Louis XIV and his fellow monarchs', in *Louis XIV and the Craft of Kingship*, ed. John C. Rule (Ohio 1969), p. 165.

18. Voltaire, *Lettres philosophiques*, I, pp. 120–2.

19. Fénelon, François Salignac de la Motte, *Examen de conscience sur les devoirs de la royauté*, printed in *Lettre à Louis XIV*, intr. Henri Guillemin (Neuchâtel 1961), pp. 104–5.

20. *Louis XIV: Mémoires, op. cit.*, p. 225.

21. For a detailed comment on Louis' memorandum, the 'Métier du roi' of 1679, see the note by Andrew Lossky in Rowen, *op. cit.*, p. 190.

22. Michel Antoine, *Le conseil du roi sous le règne de Louis XV* (Geneva 1970), pp. 48–50.

23. H. M. A. Keens-Soper, 'The French Political Academy, 1712: a school for ambassadors', *European Studies Review*, 2 (1972), 329–55; Joseph Klaits, 'Men of letters and political reform in France at the end of the reign of Louis XIV: the founding of the Académie Politique', *Journal of Modern History*, 43 (1971), 581–2, 591–2; John C. Rule, 'King and minister: Louis XIV and Colbert de Torcy', in *William III and Louis XIV*, ed. R. M. Hatton and J. S. Bromley (Liverpool 1968), p. 216.

24. Rowen, *op. cit.*, pp. 93–121. In his analysis of Louis XIV's attitude to the Spanish succession Rowen, though aware of the strategic implications, appears to discount the issue of security. Professor Hatton take a more sympathetic view of the king's defensive preoccupations while remaining critical of Louis' attitude over the War of Devolution: 'Louis XIV and his fellow monarchs', pp. 173, 178.

25. L. B. Namier, *The Structure of Politics at the Accession of George III*, 2 vols (London 1929), I, pp. 53–4. John Brooke, *The House of Commons, 1754–1790* (Oxford 1964), pp. 186–90.

26. Gruder, *op. cit.*, p. 50. Michel Antoine, *Le gouvernement et l'administration sous Louis XV* (Paris 1978), *passim*.

27. Roland E. Mousnier, 'L'évolution des institutions monarchiques en France et ses relations avec l'état social', *Le dix-septième siècle*, LVII–LIX (1963), p. 65.

28. A. Lemaire, *Les lois fondamentales de la monarchie française* (Paris 1907), pp. 42–4.

29. Sarah Hanley, *The Lit de Justice of the Kings of France* (Princeton 1983), p. 319.

30. Mousnier, *The Institutions of France under the Absolute Monarchy*, I, p. 651.

31. *Ibid*, I, p. 657.

32. Klaits, 'Men of letters and political reform in France', p. 594. Mousnier, *The Institutions of France under the Absolute Monarchy*, I, p. 656.

33. Klaits, 'Men of Letters and Political Reform in France', p. 596.

# Chapter three

# FRANCE (II):
# THE ARGUMENT JOINED

## THE IDEAS OF JOHN LAW, SUPPORTED AND CRITICIZED

Law's patron was Louis XIV's nephew, the new Regent of France (1715–23). Philippe of Orléans inaugurated a regime of free thought which inevitably cast doubt upon the validity of Divine Right kingship. He could scarcely subscribe to that doctrine himself since he harboured grave doubts about the very existence of the deity. His avant-garde attitudes shocked some of the old guard, such as Louis XIV's widow, Madame de Maintenon, in her refuge at St Cyr. But it stimulated others to challenge the tired orthodoxies of the long reign just concluded. John Law's ideas attracted Orléans' attention some time before the regency began. By June 1719, when he wrote his *Mémoire sur le denier royal*, he had already been in effective charge of the country's finances for several years.[1] In this memorandum he outlined a rationalization of politics which offered considerable attractions to a penurious government. At the same time it drove a coach and horses through the traditional order, a regimen characterized by inequality and a lack of system.

Law began with the novel assertion that a country's income and expenditure must be governed by rules and principles, and he followed this up by enunciating fourteen such rules. One of them, the sixth, is of particular interest: taxes should be imposed universally since exemptions and privileges are abuses contrary to the general good of the state and even against the true interest of those enjoying privileges. He returned to this theme several times in the course of the memorandum: 'As well as the clergy and nobility, there are an infinite number of additional privileged people so that the weight of taxation falls on the peasant and on trade, and yet it is this peasant and this trader who allow the rich and the State to exist and who for this reason ought to be cared for.' Finally, he made a very full statement:

33

> Immunities, privileges and exemptions must be regarded as abuses which cannot be abolished soon enough. Clerics, noblemen or commoners, we are all equally subjects of the same king; it is against the nature of being a subject to aspire to be distinguished from others by the privilege of not paying tribute to his prince. What I say of the comparison between subjects I will also say of provinces, and of the comparisons between them; and in particular the clergy and nobility, being the two premier orders of the kingdom, should seek to distinguish themselves by their eagerness to contribute to the expenses of the State, rather than by immunities and exemptions. Nothing is more important for the good order of a kingdom than uniformity, and it is to be wished that it should reign in laws, customs and taxes.[2]

In each of these observations Law referred to the State. But in the context of French dynasticism the question has to be posed: what kind of state could it be which had as its basis the equality of its citizens before the law and as tax-payers? Clearly if such a regime were to be imposed in France it would imply the complete rejection of any axis linking the Crown with a particular group. It would also lift on to the shoulders of government weightier powers that it had ever before contemplated. Responsibility for the well-being of each individual subject would devolve wholly upon the Crown and in that eventuality proprietorial kingship would no longer have meaning. Such a massive increase in royal authority could not be justified on traditional legal grounds, nor by resort to the title of God's lieutenant. How then might it be justified? Law hinted that the interests of the people at large might provide such a justification, though he was no more anxious than the late sixteenth-century supporters of absolute kingship to subordinate royal authority to any sort of popular control. In his 'Idée générale du nouveau système des finances', written in 1720, he observed that his new system made the prince's interests depend upon those of his subjects, but 'sans diminuer l'authorité [sic] royale'.[3]

Even Louis XIV had resorted to similarly ambiguous language in 1709 when Torcy and his royal master were forced to appeal for something approaching national support. Louis' letter to his provincial governors which was composed by Torcy in that year was designed to rally the country behind a renewed war effort made necessary by the unacceptably harsh terms laid down by the king's enemies at the peace negotiations of the Hague. 'I am persuaded that they [the people] themselves would be against receiving it [peace] upon conditions equally opposite to justice and the honour of the French name,' ran the letter, and the final two words were printed in capitals.[4]

This letter bore important overtones. The king came close to accounting to his people for the continuation of a war which, after the hard winter of 1709, had become almost unendurable. He was careful to relegate to second place the affront to dynasticism posed by the Allies' suggestion that Louis should assist in removing his grandson from the throne of Spain. Instead he concentrated on the unacceptable threat to French security implicit in the peace terms.[5] The significance of this letter lay not only in its content but equally in the widespread publicity which it received. It was printed and read throughout the country and it seems to have called forth, from civilians and the military alike, a new determination to continue the war. Shortly afterwards, in March 1713, royal letters-patent barring Louis XIV's grandson, Philip V of Spain, from ever succeeding to the French crown spoke of the people's welfare as the supreme law which the king was duty bound to obey.[6]

Such inchoate principles when logically elaborated would appear to point to one of two political conclusions. On the one hand the Crown would be forced to acknowledge its representative status vis-à-vis the people, who would presumably demonstrate their authority through institutions other than the monarchy. Alternatively, the plenitude of authority would remain with the king who would justify it by emphasizing his administrative, regulatory role as the servant of the state. In the latter case *le roi très chrétien* would have finally become *le roi bureaucrate*. The first alternative, however logically convincing, flew in the face of French experience and tradition. The centuries-old adherence to the fundamental law of succession gave the French king a title to his inheritance alongside which any other sanction for his authority still paled into insignificance. It was one thing for Louis XIV and Philip V to sign away the latter's rights in order to procure a desperately needed peace treaty. It would have been quite another for Philip to have followed up this course of action in practice, if Louis XV had died without heirs. Had not the Spanish Succession crisis itself turned upon French determination to maintain the principle that rights of succession overrode treaty renunciations? Speaking in that vein on behalf of his master, the foreign secretary, Torcy, made it clear to his English counterpart, Henry St John, Viscount Bolingbroke, during discussion leading to the Peace of Utrecht, that 'The Estates of France do not meddle in matters concerning the succession to the Crown; they lack the power to do it or to rescind laws . . . an assembly of the Estates. . . not having been called for almost a century, has in a sense been abolished in the realm.'[7]

Appeals to popular support, therefore, were largely a rhetorical device. The true language of the political establishment remained obstinately dynastic. Thus, whereas in England Robert Walpole's pamphlet of 1712 discussed *The Debts of the Nation*, a phrase which by the 1730s had been modified to the more familiar one of national debt, John Law, writing in 1720, during the brief period of his controller-generalship of finance, was still able to refer to the king's debts.[8] The second political conclusion, therefore, was the one that seemed more likely to be drawn. That implied a steady growth in royal power, justified by an increasing administrative role. Although it too was likely to be inhibited by the persistence of patrimonialism, it was a view which some Frenchmen were beginning to espouse.

Even before the end of the seventeenth century an admiralty official in Dunkirk, Pottier de la Hestroye, began to write of the state as a machine whose rhythms risked irreparable damage if interrupted.[9] The same analogy was taken up in the early eighteenth century by the *abbé* de Saint-Pierre who wrote, 'a great State can be thought of as a huge machine that the king should operate by means of different springs of various sorts. It is therefore necessary that he who is to become king know the principal parts of his machine.'[10] Thus in the spirit of Newton's newly discovered mechanistic universe, the ruler, like God himself, was to find his justification in the expertness of his maintenance work.

The Marquis d'Argenson pursued a similar line of argument. Despite the fact that he was for three years (1744–47) Louis XV's foreign secretary, d'Argenson's opinions were by no means those of the government establishment. He was a radical thinker, 'the secretary of state of the republic of Plato', as the courtier, the Duc de Richelieu, styled him.[11] D'Argenson stressed the inadequacy of the traditional arrangement between Crown and nobility, with its built-in inequalities. 'Most of our laws,' he argued, 'have been dictated by the aristocracy, and by the influence of the strongest.' While that state of affairs remained, the equality between the citizenry which would transform the power of the king's state could not be achieved. 'The nobility is too close to the throne,' he argued, 'to submit to it properly.'[12] Like John Law he saw the virtue of a basic legal equality amongst subjects, with few special concessions to wealth or social status, all united in a regime policed by an all-powerful sovereign. To describe this regime, d'Argenson too resorted to the analogy of a complex machine composed of many parts. But he also chose a horticultural image: 'A single gardener will suffice to correct, on rare occasions, those few plants that degenerate or deprive their neighbours of nourishment.'[13] In either guise, as skilled technician or green-fingered gardener, the king tended to stand outside the system which he serviced, the state which he regulated and served. But in doing so he had to maintain the loyalty and respect of his subjects: they had to accept willingly the additional powers wielded by the king as first servant of the state. They would be persuaded to do so by the acquisition of that liberty which the new authority of the state would provide, a liberty less preserved by it than in its gift: 'Freedom is the Throne's support; order makes freedom legitimate.'[14]

Yet d'Argenson was also the representative of a distinguished noble house, and a pragmatist. Though nobility ought not to exist, though every citizen should receive his rewards through talent and not through privilege, that was not, sadly, the way of the world. Every effort should be made to seek equality, and in the process of doing so, at least to prevent the number of nobles from increasing. But as for 'an absolute and Platonic equality? Certainly not.'[15]

Although in his later years d'Argenson became somewhat equivocal in his view of the role of the nobility in the French state, he was clearly opposed to the conservative *thèse nobiliaire*. This thesis was magisterially expounded by his contemporary, another distinguished lawyer and nobleman, the Baron de la Brède et de Montesquieu in his *De l'esprit des lois* of 1748. It was Montesquieu's views, not d'Argenson's, that matched the French tradition and gave *De l'esprit des lois* its beacon quality in the darkening years before the Revolution. Montesquieu's was the true voice of the French political establishment. He endorsed more powerfully than ever before the interlocking relationship of government and property-owners at the heart of the *ancien régime*. He identified the concept of honour as the motive force behind the arrangement, defining it in terms of the quest for preference and distinction. Although he wrote of intermediate, subordinate and dependent powers, there can be no doubt that for him true monarchical authority could only be exercised as a partnership: 'in a kind of way, nobility enters into the essence of monarchy'.[16] He warned against abolishing the prerogatives of the seigneurs, the nobility, the clergy and the towns, for that would be to embark on the road to despotism. Despotism for Montesquieu was political equality, equal subjection to government caprice. Therefore he castigated John Law as 'one of the greatest promoters of despotism yet seen in Europe. As well as the sudden, unusual and outrageous changes which he introduced, he wanted to remove the intermediate ranks and destroy the political order.'[17] Montesquieu was standing d'Argenson's dictum, 'freedom is the Throne's support; order makes freedom legitimate', precisely on its head.

Thus, by the mid-eighteenth century the battle was joined. It was not yet on the streets of the capital between revolutionaries and conservatives, but in Parisian *salons* between the powdered representatives of two schools of thought which may, in pre-1789 terms, be similarly categorized. Although in his writings Montesquieu shared the contemporary fashion for mechanistic metaphors, he did not envisage the state as an independent force justifying government action. On the contrary, since his own concern was to limit the opportunities for despotism his view of the monarchical state paid less attention to the king's role as administrator and more to his possessory function, implying as it did the maintenance of a contract between the Crown and the owners of property.

## THE *PARLEMENT* OF PARIS

Montesquieu's ideas, even his language, were eagerly seized upon by the most articulate and best organized spokesmen of one of the contracting parties, the noble magistrates of the *Parlement* of Paris. As pressure mounted for the establishment of a more highly regulated regime, a 'police state' in eighteenth-century terms, so the conservative opposition sought stronger ideological weapons with which to defend themselves. It was becoming possible to consider the interests of the people as detached from those of the Crown, and provided that these interests could be harnessed within the established hierarchical relationships they could powerfully reinforce the *status quo*. Montesquieu himself gave the lead to the magistrates. He linked his concept of intermediary ranks in the state to the existence of a *dépôt des lois*, 'which proclaims laws when they are made, and recalls them when they are forgotten'. In addition, his magnum opus was a sociological as well as a legal tract. In the preface to *De l'esprit des lois* he reminded his readers, 'J'ai d'abord examiné les hommes.'[18] The language of that examination was also borrowed by the Parisian judges.

An analysis of the politico-judicial complaints or remonstrances of the *Parlement* during the eighteenth century reveals the court's attempts to preserve the established order by giving to old arguments a new linguistic complexion.[19] The magistrates' political conservatism was reflected in the patrimonial view of kingship which persisted in their remonstrances throughout the century. The familiar metaphors of paternal authority and headship of the body politic were invoked, together with references to the king's *gloire*, and the complementary theme of divine right. As late as 1770 the court recorded the conventional formula: 'Les rois sont les images de Dieu sur la terre.' It was not to be expected that this conservative view would permit the concept of an equal relationship between Crown and subjects. Nor did it: the remonstrances are littered with references to 'the orders of the kingdom', 'all the orders which make up your monarchy'. In 1776, the *Parlement*'s *avocat-général*, Séguier, elaborated upon the subject:

> All your subjects, Sire, are divided into as many different bodies as there are conditions in the Kingdom: Clergy, Nobility, sovereign courts, lower tribunals, the officers attached to these tribunals, universities, academies, financial companies, commercial companies, all of them represent, throughout the State, living bodies which may be regarded as links in a great chain the first of which is held by Your Majesty, as head and sovereign administrator of the whole body of the Nation.[20]

Yet a subtle change was nevertheless taking place in *parlementaire* vocabulary. Take, for example, the word 'nation'. At the beginning of Louis XV's reign the interests of the nation were conventionally thought of as coinciding with those of the Crown. There appeared to be no political role for the nation which could not be and was not expressed through the sovereign. The magistrates acknowledged this state of affairs from time to time: 'the interests of your people, inseparable from those of Your Majesty', 'the public good and the interest of your service from which it is inseparable'. Such protestations of orthodoxy however did not always reflect the court's attitude. Then Louis XV found it necessary to compel the judges to acknowledge that the king alone possessed absolute power for the exercise of which he was accountable only to God; that the bond uniting king and nation was indissoluble. That was in 1766; by 1787 the *Parlement* was denying the capacity of royal legislation to deprive the nation of its rights.[21]

Such a change in emphasis necessarily affected the concept of estates and orders, for if the umbilical cord uniting the subjects to the Crown were to be severed, the relationship of those subjects to the ruler would have to be redefined. The result was the appearance in *parlementaire* remonstrances of the word 'society', meaning the totality of the subjects and implying their equal relationship as individuals to the Crown, as opposed to membership of juridical groupings. Significantly, in the light of the publication date of Montesquieu's *De l'esprit des lois*, this new usage can only be discerned from the 1750s, as can the investing of the word 'men' with a universal significance: 'The desire for independence, Sire, is born with all men.' For the remainder of the *Parlement*'s existence it interwove in its remonstrances, alongside expressions of unimpeachable orthodoxy, novel linguistic implications attaching to 'humanity' and 'society'. In January 1779 the judges wrote of the 'rights of humanity'; in March 1788 they claimed that 'the nature of man is to be united to his fellow men and to live in society'.[22]

It was a similar story with the word 'property' which was introduced into the *Parlement*'s remonstrances in the 1780s in the guise of an inalienable and universal right, a great principle 'which makes of man a citizen and of all the citizens a State, and which, supported by law, upholds the whole mass of the social body'. More cryptically, in April 1788, they asserted that 'every citizen possesses property; if he is poor he at least has his liberty'.[23]

'Liberty' too underwent something of a metamorphosis in *parlementaire* hands. It began the eighteenth century as the equivalent of 'liberties', meaning the lawful rights and privileges enjoyed by particular groups, thus confirming the concept of an unequal, corporate regime, its inequalities legally guaranteed. The liberty owed by princes to their subjects, therefore, as the bishop of Clermont reminded the young king Louis XV in 1718, was simply the liberty that the law provided.[24] By the second half of the century, however, an artful mutation was affecting the sense of 'liberty' in some of the court's remonstrances. As with their novel interpretation of 'men' and 'society', the magistrates began to apply the quality of universality to the word 'liberty'. 'Every citizen by his birth in a monarchy has a right to his legitimate liberty,' they protested in 1764. By 1788 they were proclaiming liberty to be the imprescriptible right of each individual citizen and observing in a manifestly derivative phrase that 'man is born free and his happiness rests on justice'.[25] On one level the *Parlement* was doing no more than re-affirming its ancient principle that government should be regulated by the law. Yet the emphasis had subtly changed over the course of the century: the concept of specific rights for legally constituted groups was threatening to fade before that of the universal rights of man.

Here we touch closely on the central theme of this book. Was political liberty only to be found in the destruction of sectional liberties? If so, by what power were the latter to be swept away, and with what justification? If liberty was a natural human right the political order must surely reflect that fact. Yet such a passive role did not match the reality of eighteenth-century government which was moving towards a policy of greater regulation and control of the subjects' lives. Alternatively, therefore, liberty might have to be sought in the canons of the all-powerful state.

Faced by the alarming growth in administrative government which threatened to undermine the legal status quo of which the *Parlement* was the chief institutional guardian, the magistrates were guilty of using borrowed ammunition to fight their cause, and eventually it blew up in their faces. From time to time they made it plain that fundamentally their position had not changed. So in March 1776 their remonstrances solemnly warned that:

> any system which under an appearance of humanity and beneficence
> might lead to the establishment between men of an equality of duties and
> to the destruction of necessary distinctions would soon cause disorder, the
> inevitable result of absolute equality, and the overthrow of civil society,
> whose harmony depends upon the gradation of powers, authorities,
> preeminences and distinctions which keep everyone in his place.

At the very end of the court's life, as its members came to realize that implications could be drawn from their own arguments and meanings attached to their own vocabulary which threatened to undermine the whole legal edifice of the *ancien régime*, the remonstrances became doom-laden: 'endeavours are being made to establish a system of equality, as if it were possible to realize such an idea. This speculation, vain though it is, sows the germ of anarchy among the citizens; it will bring about the ruin of royal authority, destroying at the same time all civil and monarchic order.'[26]

But it was too late. The magistrates' attempt to fight the growth of a regulatory state served by the king as its chief bureaucrat, by espousing the nation's cause, opened the way to the logical alternative of an 'English' solution in which the state's authority would derive from other institutions than that of the monarchy alone. When in September 1788 the *Parlement* of Paris registered the royal declaration summoning the first meeting of the Estates-General since 1614, it made clear the fact that voting would be by estate in the traditional manner, and not by individual voice. Ordinary Parisians who had cheered the magistrates as heroes against royal oppression in the preceding months underwent a rapid change of heart. They perceived the *parlementaires* as the stubborn, legalistic representatives of an unchanging regime. The court's decision effectively marked the beginning of the end of the old order. The powerlessness and irrelevance of the ancient contract between Crown and property was suddenly rendered apparent. The question of what was to take its place both precipitated and sustained the Revolution.

## COMMISSIONERS VERSUS OFFICE-HOLDERS

The financial realities with which French governments had to grapple during the eighteenth century ranged its non-office-holding servants ineluctably against the *thèse parlementaire*. Though Montesquieu's vision was less fanciful than those of earlier aristocratic supporters of a narrow union between Crown and nobility, writers like Fénelon, Boulainvilliers and Saint-Simon, it was nevertheless far removed from the actual situation facing the government. Following the mirage of economic recovery under John Law, the old fiscal problems returned. For a time it appeared that Law's policy of encouraging economic growth by the introduction of paper money and the establishment of a national trading company had revitalized the French economy and removed the government's financial worries. However, a frenzied period of speculation followed, leading to hyper-inflation and the inevitable crash. The king's agents were driven to contemplate other drastic solutions to their problems and in doing so put ever more grievous stress upon existing loyalties.

Already in 1710 Louis XIV had been obliged to introduce the *dixième*, a temporary wartime tax to be levied on all his subjects, noble and non-noble alike. A 10 per cent levy was imposed on all property, including offices. The *dixième* was re-imposed in 1733 during the War of the Polish Succession and again in 1741 in the War of the Austrian Succession. From 1749 landowners had intermittently to bear the *vingtième* tax, a 5 per cent levy which replaced the *dixième*. Apart from the reduced taxation rate the new tax differed only in one respect from its predecessor. It was however a crucial difference, for the *vingtième* was introduced in peacetime, without the excuse of a temporary crisis to justify such a levy. With the outbreak of the Seven Years' War in 1756 the government's financial demands became even more oppressive. A second twentieth was introduced in that year and a third in 1760, both to last for the duration of the war and to be paid by all the king's subjects except the clergy, who had succeeded in 1751 in acquiring exemption.

Noble loyalties were strained not only by the introduction of new fiscal obligations but also by the manner in which increasingly financial matters were regulated. In his meticulous and definitive analysis of the royal council under Louis XV, Michel Antoine draws attention to the fact that the number of financial decrees issued between 1715 and 1774 was out of all proportion to the diminishing number of sessions held by the royal council of finance during the reign.[27] It appears that many financial decrees were promulgated as a result of the weekly discussions between the controller-general and his professional advisers. The latter were acquiring the sort of expertise during this period that we nowadays associate with permanent government officials.[28] The government servants appointed by royal commission had far more flexibility and freedom of action than had the king's office-holders who had purchased a specific function. But the fact that the king's service contained both kinds of official made the achievement of a full-blooded administrative transformation virtually impossible. Rivalry between the two kinds of official was not, of course, the only reason for that failure. The *Parlement* regularly sniped at 'le despotisme anonyme des commis', and especially at the fiscal activities of those 'administrateurs despotiques', the provincial intendants.[29] It did so in support of the widely held opinion that efficient government was no substitute for legitimate government. The Parisian *cour des aides*, headed by the great Malesherbes, put the matter succinctly in its remonstrances of 1761: 'Administration linked with jurisdiction will always produce despotism because the citizens' security consists in being judged by those who recognize no other ruling principle than the law; whereas the dubious principles of administration readily serve to add weight to injustice.'[30]

This view, which underlines the survival capacity of the possessory, dynastic idea of kingship in France, was enthusiastically endorsed by Louis XV.[31] This was despite the fact that his officials were busily engaged in demonstrating the effectiveness of the alternative model, that of administrative kingship. The credibility gap which thus emerged served to encourage further the critics of the so-called tyranny of the commissioners. Consequently, it became more difficult for the Crown to implement necessary reform, enmeshed as it was in a web of inherited legal constraints. Louis XV himself regularly asserted the personal authority of his forbears. He did so unequivocally, for instance, in his reproof to the *Parlement* of Paris, delivered in March 1766 at the famous *séance de la flagellation*, when he pronounced that 'sovereign power, whose proper nature consists of the spirit of counsel, justice and reason, resides exclusively in my person; . . . the rights and interests of the Nation, the latter audaciously envisaged as a body distinct from the Monarch, are necessarily united with mine and rest only in my hands'.[32] While such principles continued to be adduced there was scant likelihood that an impersonal state, regulated by the king and his administrators, could command the loyalty of French subjects.

## THE PHYSIOCRATIC EXPERIMENT

The same personal principle undermined the experiment in financial reform prompted by Physiocratic ideas. By a declaration of May 1763 and an edict of July 1764, Louis XV's administration introduced a novel provisioning regime. The movement of grain was to be freed entirely from controls and it was to be allowed to circulate throughout the country and beyond the frontiers without hindrance. In addition, all citizens, whatever their status, were to be allowed to participate in the grain trade. By thus reinvigorating French agriculture, the government hoped to increase the country's wealth and, consequently, by means of taxation, to make more money available for its needs.

However, in the words of the latest historian of this radical experiment, 'liberalization . . . marked a decisive rupture with one of the great monarchical traditions'.[33] At the heart of French patrimonial kingship lay the assumption that, as father of his people, the king would always intervene to ensure that his subjects did not starve. For without an adequate level of subsistence for the people, law and order could not be maintained.

It quickly became clear that if the king did not intervene the Physiocratic free market forces would cause serious problems for the poor. As early as July 1763, a senior royal official in the *Parlement* of Paris, Joly de Fleury, described the new arrangements as a recipe for social disorganization.[34] In the following years his gloomy prophecy was fulfilled. Grain riots swept the country from Normandy to the Dauphiné. Scarcity brought high prices and resentment against the merchants suspected of keeping grain away from the market in order to inflate prices further. As in England, there was evidence that local authorities were often unwilling to react in draconian fashion against the rioters. Indeed, many of them perceived the legislation as an unwarrantable assault upon public order. They looked to the king to resume his traditional responsibility for providing for the people's subsistence. Typical were the municipal officials at Châlons-sur- Marne who protested that

> It is still true that the king is the common father to his subjects and that his heart is revolted by the idea that a part of those who have the good fortune to live under his laws be exposed to lacking bread by the impossibility of meeting the price to which grain would be carried by the continuation of exports.

Ominously, though, posters began to appear in Paris, like the one in October 1768, which attacked Louis for abdicating the responsibilities traditionally associated with paternalistic kingship. Two months later the *Parlement* of Paris added its voice in favour of the king's 'affection paternelle', of which the people were being deprived.[35] Eventually, in December 1778, the then controller-general of finance, *abbé* Terray, brought the experiment to an end. Its failure ushered in a period of increased government intervention and control.

We have already observed how, in the impersonal political environment which characterized the British system, ideas of free trade seemed the natural ally of liberty and progress. It was possible to play down the lurking primacy of the state because although the impersonal concept justified intervention at any time and in any area in which the citizen had an interest, that potential was masked from day-to-day life by the elusive nature of sovereignty. In the French system the king's authority was directly engaged in the regulation of the subjects' lives. His guarantee validated all the local idiosyncracies of the various regions, the rights and privileges of municipalities and office-holders, the daunting system of internal customs barriers, all the legal minutiae which tended to restrict the development of French economic life. The Physiocrats, however, made few allowances for such facts. They shared the views of Smith and Ferguson that they were living in an age of progress in which, beyond its general provision of security, government should act chiefly to secure the rights of men of property. Their most distinguished representative, Anne-Robert-Jacques Turgot, expressed the opinion in 1763 that

Only the owner of real property is liable to contribute to taxation; a first ground for this is that he alone has a stake in the preservation of an abiding social order. What does it matter to a working man what becomes of the government? He would always own the same resources in the form of his arms; he is perfectly indifferent as to whether it is Jack or Peter who furnishes the work.[36]

Beyond the 'preservation of an abiding social order', the state should not concern itself with seeking to regulate a country's economic development, a task far more effectively accomplished by unfettered private enterprise: 'in all respects in which commerce may interest the state', wrote Turgot in his 1759 work *In Praise of Gournay*, 'unrestrained individual interest will always produce the public welfare more surely than the operations of government, which are always faulty and of necessity directed by a hazy and dubious theory'.[37] It is not surprising that such views, which were fundamentally at odds with established political and economic principles, could not be grafted successfully on to the ailing body politic of late *ancien régime* France.

## THE DUTCH ANALOGY

In France the Physiocrats' view accorded with neither the possessory nor the administrative strand in the monarchical tradition. Instead it pre-supposed a sophisticated and impersonal sovereign, who, like Voltaire's deity in respect to the creation of the universe, withdrew from the mundane arena once the state's parameters had been established. It was a doctrine more at home in London and Edinburgh. At first glance it would also appear to have a natural home in the Hague.

The Dutch Republic indeed offers an instructive analogy with France, and it was a regime which, upon closer examination, turns out to be very different from the British system. It is true that, like the British model, direct personal authority was lacking in the United Provinces, but the power of the Estates-General fell far short of that exercised by the British Parliament. For although the Estates-General acted on behalf of the Republic, signed its treaties and appointed its ambassadors, it did not possess sovereign power. That authority did not exist on the level of federal government, precisely because it was retained by those provincial elements which made up the whole Republic. Nor were there but seven sovereigns, one for each province. William Temple observed of the seventeenth-century Dutch state that,

> Each of these provinces is likewise composed of many little states or cities, which have several marks of sovereign power within themselves, and are not subject to the sovereignty of their province; not being concluded in many things by the majority, but only by the universal concurrence of voices in the provincial-states.[38]

This tradition of unanimity at all levels of government inhibited the growth of a unified political system at the provincial, as well as at the state, level. Even the most powerful province, Holland, 'was more or less a league of eighteen city-republics'.[39]

For the Dutch, as for the French Physiocrats, liberty meant the freedom to put trading and commercial interests before any other political consideration, and liberties were the rights enjoyed by men of property. Each province, each city, each group of wealthy patricians sought primarily to maintain their liberties, insisting upon a unanimity which frustrated the emergence of sovereign power at the federal level in the shape of the House of Orange. Monarchical government was per-ceived as detrimental to trade, so that even Holland, which contributed 16 per cent more than the other provinces combined to the federal revenue, was prepared to put up with the obstructive behaviour of far weaker allies in the federation in order to defeat that possibility.[40] So long as the Republic prospered, its shaky political foundations could be concealed – and at moments of crisis the House of Orange might be allowed briefly to resume its protective military role. But that prosperity began to fail with the prolonged wars against Louis XIV and Britain's emergence as the world's leading commercial power. A policy of free trade at all costs, when practised in a period of reduced competitiveness, began to look like political suicide. John Law noted the dangers of such economic profligacy as early as 1716, and for much of the following century the Republic's business interests dictated that Dutch capital should be invested in England.[41] The result was, as Wallerstein puts it, that 'The symbiotic arrangement between a formerly hegemonic power and the new rising star provided graceful retirement income for the one and a crucial push forward against its rival for the other.'[42] More to the point of the present essay, this symbiotic relationship demonstrated the ineffectiveness of economic freedom as the basis of political organization when challenged by the power of impersonal state sovereignty.

It was late in the eighteenth century, at the climax of the Patriotic Revolt of the 1780s, before the liberties enshrined in the Union of Utrecht of 1579 were brought into question. The domination of the upper middle class had been tightening since the end of the Eighty Years' War against Spain (1568–1648) when the urban elite of Holland had first become entrenched in the governing offices of its chief towns. Between 1650 and 1750 these oligarchies succeeded in restricting membership of the important civil offices to an ever narrower group of families. From 1698 to 1748 the senior offices of Amsterdam were monopolized by just forty regents. So-called contracts of correspondence were drawn up between them to offer reciprocal aid in procuring promotion and co-option to high offices as they became available.[43]

As in France, therefore, offices became venal and hereditary, a state of affairs which further militated against political reform or a widening of those liberties on which the Union had been based. Unlike the situation in France, with its bifurcated tradition of proprietorial and administrative kingship, there was no alternative political tradition in the history of the Dutch Republic which could be exploited in order to challenge the power of the urban oligarchs. Despite the efforts of political commentators like Ulric Huber to elaborate a more sophisticated relationship between government and subjects, the prevailing ideology was one grounded in the ultimate supremacy of commercial liberties.[44] It was to be expected therefore that such a political order would become increasingly exclusive in the absence of a state sovereign to insist, in the interests of the subjects at large, upon a greater degree of equality between them. Thus even the reform movement towards the end of the eighteenth century remained wedded to the federal principle upon which the Republic's old glories had been based. Only after 1795, the year in which the French revolutionary armies entered Holland, did the process of radical political change become inescapable.

In France there was too much political control to allow the physiocratic experiment to succeed. In the Dutch Republic, by contrast, there was too little to guarantee the stability and security necessary for flourishing economic life. Britain, uniquely, evolved a subtle relationship between sovereign power and economic freedom which was capable of converting the principles of laissez-faire into a realistic political doctrine.[45]

# REFERENCES AND NOTES

1. J. H. Shennan, *Philippe Duke of Orléans: Regent of France 1715–1723* (London 1979), pp. 108 ff.
2. The *mémoire* is printed in *John Law, oeuvres complètes*, ed. P. Harsin, 3 vols (Paris 1934), III, pp. 39–61.
3. Law, 'Idée générale du nouveau système des finances', *op. cit.*, III, p. 89.
4. Joseph Klaits, *Printed Propoganda under Louis XIV* (Princeton 1976), pp. 216–17. Klaits prints the whole letter on pp. 214–16.
5. R. M. Hatton, 'Louis XIV and his Fellow Monarchs', in *Louis XIV and the Craft of Kingship*, ed. John C. Rule (Ohio 1969), p. 179.
6. Klaits, *Printed Propaganda*, p. 290.
7. Printed in the documentary collection edited by Orest and Patricia Ranum, *The Century of Louis XIV* (London 1973), p. 459.
8. P. G. M. Dickson, *The Financial Revolution in England* (London 1967), p. 50. Law, 'Idée générale du nouveau système des finances', *op cit.*, III, p. 95.
9. Lionel Rothkrug, *Opposition to Louis XIV: the political and social origins of the French Enlightenment* (Princeton 1965), p. 440.
10. Nannerl O. Keohane, *Philosophy and the State in France* (Princeton 1980), p. 371, note 28.
11. L. Lanier, 'Le club de l'entresol (1723–1731)', *Mémoires de l'académie des sciences, des lettres et des arts d'Amiens*, 3me série, VI (1879), p. 32.
12. Marquis d'Argenson, *Journal et mémoires*, ed. E. J. B. Rathery, 9 vols (Paris 1859–67), I, pp. 373–4.
13. Keohane, *op. cit.*, pp. 386, 389.
14. Marquis d'Argenson, *Considérations sur le gouvernement ancien et présent de la France* (Amsterdam 1764), p. 316.
15. *Ibid.*, p. 310.
16. Baron de Montesquieu, *De l'esprit des lois*, in *Oeuvres complètes*, ed. du Seuil (Paris 1964), Book 2, ch. 4, p. 535.
17. *Ibid.*, Book 2, Ch. 4, pp. 535–6.
18. *Ibid.*, preface, p. 529.
19. J. H. Shennan, 'The political vocabulary of the Parlement of Paris in the eighteenth century', *Atti del quarto congresso internazionale della società italiana di storia del diritto* (Florence 1982), II, 951–64.
20. J. Flammermont, *Remontrances du parlement de Paris au XVIII^e siècle*, 3 vols (Paris 1888–98), III, pp. 168, 345–6.
21. *Ibid.*, II, p. 563; III, p. 692.
22. *Ibid.*, I, p. 530; III, pp. 448, 715.
23. *Ibid.*, III, pp. 612–13, 738.
24. J. B. Massillon, *Oeuvres complètes*, 13 vols (Paris 1822–25), VI, p. 130.
25. Flammermont, *op. cit.*, II, p. 473; III, pp. 713–14.
26. *Ibid.*, III, pp. 279, 796.
27. Antoine, *Le conseil du roi*, pp. 384 ff.
28. We must beware, however, of exaggerating their professionalism. See the comments of Clive H. Church, *Revolution and Red Tape: the French ministerial bureaucracy, 1770–1850* (Oxford 1981), pp. 21–2.

29.  Jean Egret, *Louis XV et l'opposition parlementaire* (Paris 1970), pp. 116, 119.
30.  Antoine, *Le conseil du roi*, pp. 415–16.
31.  Sarah Hanley, *The Lit de Justice of the Kings of France* (Princeton 1983), p. 341.
32.  Flammermont, *op. cit.*, II, pp. 557–8.
33.  S. L. Kaplan, *Bread, Politics and Political Economy in the Reign of Louis XV*, 2 vols (The Hague 1976), I, p. 163.
34.  *Ibid.*, I. p. 172.
35.  *Ibid.*, I, pp. 202, 320; Flammermont, *op. cit.*, III, p. 21.
36.  *The Economics of A. R. J. Turgot*, ed. P. D. Groenewegen (The Hague 1977): 'Plan for a paper on taxation in general, on land taxes in particular, and on the project of a land register' (1763), p. 106.
37.  *The Economics of A. R. J. Turgot*, 'In praise of Gournay' (1759), p. 29. See too the writings of *Turgot on Progress, Sociology and Economics*, ed. Ronald L. Meek (Cambridge 1973).
38.  William Temple, *Observations upon the United Provinces of the Netherlands* (London 1673), p. 75.
39.  H. Wansink, 'Holland and six allies: the Republic of the Seven United Provinces', *Britain and the Netherlands,* IV, ed. J. S. Bromley and E. H. Kossman (The Hague 1971), p. 136.
40.  E. H. Kossmann, 'The crisis of the Dutch state, 1780–1813: nationalism, federalism, unitarism', *Britain and the Netherlands*, IV, p. 159. G. J. Renier, *The Dutch Nation* (London 1944), p. 22.
41.  Law, 'Mémoire sur la politique monétaire française', *op. cit.*, II, p. 324.
42.  Immanuel Wallerstein, *The Modern World System*, vol II: *Mercantilism and the Consolidation of the European World Economy*, 1600–1750 (London 1980), p. 281.
43.  S. Schama, *Patriots and Liberators: revolution in the Netherlands, 1780–1813* (London 1977), p. 55.
44.  E. H. Kossmann, 'The development of Dutch political theory in the seventeenth century', *Britain and the Netherlands* ed. J. S. Bromley and E. H. Kossmann (London 1960), pp. 109–10.
45.  Note the interesting observations on the varieties of economic freedom and control in the three countries during the seventeenth century, in Roland Mousnier, *Les XVI<sup>e</sup> et XVII<sup>e</sup> siècles* (Paris 1961), pp. 258 ff.

*Chapter four*

# FRANCE (III): THE FATE OF THE HOUSE OF BOURBON

## GOVERNMENT REFORM AND VACILLATION

The failure of the physiocratic experiment in the late 1760s coincided with the French government's momentous decision to reform the sovereign courts. For a number of years the government's commissioners had been clashing with its venal office-holders, especially over tax-raising policies. The courts stood halfway between the Physiocrats and the supporters of an administrative regime and fell before the counter-attack of the *commis*. In January 1771 the government moved to silence its most persistent critics. Frustrated by their censorious disposition, the chancellor, Maupeou, deprived the magistrates in the *Parlement* of Paris of their offices and sent them into provincial exile. In April the king presided over the establishment of a new judicial body to take the place of the recalcitrant court. Three other *parlements*, those of Rouen, Douai and Metz, were abolished, as well as the outspoken *cour des aides* in Paris. The remainder were remodelled. This was the government's most drastic attempt since the days of John Law to gain greater freedom of action. Not only were the sovereign courts abolished or transformed: the new magistrates could no longer buy their offices and could therefore be dismissed more readily than their predecessors.

Between 1771 and Louis XV's death in 1774 the new regime afforded a tranquil dénouement to the reign. Terray's tax reforms – the reduction of interest rates and the prolongation of the *vingtième* – caused relatively few difficulties: 'For the first time in years the government did not have to bargain over its financial policy.'[1] All the old controls over the circulation of grain were restored and the king's obligation to intervene firmly restated. Terray further tightened his control by proposing a comprehensive scheme for the collection of data to inform central government policy on subsistence; and by investing the intendants with new judicial powers to deal with those who defied the policy on grain. The *Parlement* of Toulouse was firmly told in November 1772 that the king's policy had to be both paternalistic and interventionist, formulated in accordance with his perception of the public interest.[2] Though the two aspects of kingship, the proprietorial and the administrative, were thus united, it seemed clear at this stage that the *roi bureaucrate* was edging out his patrimonial rival.

However, that development never came about, in part because of royal ambivalence.[3] A few months after Louis XV's death, his grandson, Louis XVI, a conventional man, reverted to long-standing practice. He dismissed the reforming chancellor, Maupeou, and within a year the new regime had been totally dismantled. In retrospect it seemed a fatal decision, for its effect was to restore the equilibrium within government between two conflicting philosophies, thereby increasing tensions and removing the possibility of effective action. Between 1771 and 1781, chiefly under the direction of Jacques Necker, progress was made in converting *ad hoc* fiscal methods into fully fledged bureaucratic procedures. The venal offices of intendant of finance were temporarily suppressed and their work taken over by an important committee, the *comité contentieux des finances*. That was one aspect of a determined endeavour to establish a system of public finance whereby the collection, management and spending of revenue were closely supervised by the government. The importance of private financial agents in the system was thereby much reduced. This policy was pursued further in the Treasury reforms of 1788, directed by Loménie de Brienne.[4]

However, such initiatives continued to encounter an implacable bedrock opposition based upon venality, patronage and a society of orders, all of them the concomitants of personal kingship. In April 1775 the newly restored Parisian *cour des aides* complained bitterly to the king on the subject of fiscal legislation, that 'It cannot be said that it is the council of Your Majesty itself that renders such decrees, for we affirm a notorious fact in saying that the council never hears them mentioned.'[5] It appeared, in the words of the most recent historian of the French bureaucracy, that the *ancien régime* 'was not able to resolve the ultimate dilemma of social privileges and exception on which it had deliberately been built in the first place'.[6] That principle of inequality was juridically enshrined in the three estates of the realm, just as the principle of juridical equality was at the root of the English parliamentary system. But whereas Adam Ferguson could convincingly gloss over that basic equality to point up the evident inequalities between subjects, it was far more difficult for a French commentator to discern signs of equality between subjects and to discount their fundamental inequality. The reason is once more to be found in the distinction between the personal contract between Crown and nobility on the one hand, and the elusive, impersonal sovereignty buried in the relationship of crown, lords and commons on the other.

But that personal contract was rapidly losing its appeal to representatives of both parties. In June 1789, when few people were any longer listening seriously to what he said, Louis XVI re-affirmed the Crown's commitment to the preservation of the three orders of the kingdom 'as essentially inherent in the constitution'. This opinion had also been expressed in the previous autumn by the *Parlement* of Paris.[7] However, by that time, the final attempt at renegotiation had already failed.

In 1786 the controller-general of finance, Charles de Calonne, introduced his plan for financial reform. This plan was not perceived as being revolutionary. It was, however, a radical programme containing elements of the physiocratic ideas of earlier years. Its central plank, the proposal to introduce a tax on all landowners, whatever their status, bore a striking resemblance to John Law's plan of 1719, contained in his *Mémoire sur le denier royal*. In addition, Calonne proposed to dismantle internal customs barriers and once more to instal a regime of free trade in grain. The Assembly of Notables that was summoned to receive and endorse his proposals embarked upon a serious and prolonged analysis of them. The failure to reach agreement may be partly accounted for by Calonne's lack of political tact. Only partly, however; for at the heart of the disagreement lay the antithesis between administrative and proprietorial monarchy which was now threatening the very survival of the old order.

Calonne had made his reputation as an intendant. That office empowered him to override and supervise the decisions of a variety of legally constituted local authorities in the interests of the central government. He was therefore a representative of that 'royal despotism' so feared by the social establishment. He had shown himself willing, in the interests of the state's fiscal needs, to reduce all the nation's liberties to an unwanted equality. Equality is all very well in republics and in Philadelphia, commented the archbishop of Toulouse, Loménie de Brienne, who succeeded the disgraced Calonne in 1788, and it may be appropriate to despotisms and Constantinople; but in France the *Grands* are at one and the same time the people's support and the monarchy's.[8] Montesquieu could not have put it better.

There appeared to be no means of resolving the dilemma of how to renegotiate the contract to take into account changed and changing circumstances. Calonne's was but the latest, and as it turned out, the last attempt to adapt the French political system to eighteenth-century realities. It failed in part because the choice was becoming all too clear.

By 1789 there was a good deal of agreement about the theoretical and practical needs of French government. The needs of security clearly dictated that power at the centre should be tightened, an aim that could best be achieved by equalizing the relationship between the government and each citizen individually. It has been remarked earlier that France's logical political development during the eighteenth century appeared to be via one of two alternatives: either by the establishment of representative bodies to act alongside the Crown, or by the emergence of an administrative monarchy whose regulatory function would be sufficient justification for its sovereignty. The first alternative was not a practical proposition in the light of the powerful monarchical tradition which in the early modern period had subsumed all its rivals. Indeed, that same tradition also militated against the implementation of the second alternative. For French government remained essentially personal, and it was the impersonality of sovereign power that gave the state its overwhelming authority. Such authority when claimed by the Crown alone smacked of tyranny, and was far more likely to be resisted than accepted in a country where political power was exercised and limited by means of the legal relationships between the king and the hierarchy of his subjects, 'without which monarchy can nowhere exist'.[9]

It is not surprising therefore that the government's strenuous efforts to assert greater administrative control should have been branded as despotic. The fact was that liberty seemed to be more firmly assured when it was dependent upon the arbitrary and all-pervading power of the impersonal state than when it had to rely upon the limited authority of dynastic monarchy. Eighteenth-century ideas of progress, liberty and equality grew under the lengthening shadow of the impersonal state idea whose primacy may be taken as axiomatic even in the libertarian doctrines of the Scottish Enlightenment.

## IDEAS OF LIBERTY AND EQUALITY

Since the system based on inequality was proving unworkable, it was not surprising that a new regime based on equality should start to beckon, articulated in the beguiling language of political liberty. We have already noted the powerful contribution of eighteenth-century history writing to the pursuit of that ideal, and the self-deceiving efforts of the magistrates of the Paris *Parlement* to adapt the new ideas to old purposes. Among the latter's long-standing adversaries, the *commissaires départis* or intendants, there were some who showed more genuine enthusiasm than either their royal master or his chief judges for the alternative system. They wrote approvingly of the love of liberty and disapprovingly of the oppressive rights of privilege and immunity. The intendant of Alsace, Chaumont de la Galaizière, maintained that, 'The constitution of States cannot be absolutely fixed and permanent. The times, the progress of enlightenment, changes in customs and opinions, lead to and necessitate revolutions in the political system of governments . . . Today every citizen desires a summons to contribute to the general good. This frame of mind cannot be encouraged too much.' At Bordeaux, Dupré de Saint-Maur spoke of the 'many nobles and privileged persons . . . of the immunities granted to them, so crushing and humiliating for the ordinary people'. The intendant of Provence, Des Gallois de la Tour, called Louis XVI 'this citizen king' and apostrophized the estates of Provence thus: 'Clergy, Nobility, Third Estate, here you are but Citizens.'[10]

Like the intendants, the high priests of the French Enlightenment contributed to the growing debate on equality. They found the answer in the concept of 'society'. From the middle years of the century this idea provided the chief intellectual justification for the elaboration of a new political order. It was treated extensively by Denis Diderot in the *Encyclopédie*, that pure fountain of enlightened opinion. Diderot's views are interesting. He limited man's equality to that of the shared human condition, leaving out of account differences in wealth and status. His reasoning was that *sub specie aeternitatis* such inequalities were superficial. Since societies were established in the first place to procure the individual's happiness, an equal obligation fell upon all of its members. Indeed, to provide for the mutual security which was the first objective of his political design, Diderot positively insisted upon the need for unequal contributions: 'la subordination est le lien de la société, et que sans cela il n'y aurait aucun ordre dans les familles, ni dans le gouvernement civil'.[11]

The liberty of the individual citizen was interpreted by Diderot, as by Montesquieu, as the right to do whatever the law allowed. But how was this overarching societal interest to be defined and enforced if, as Diderot himself admitted in a separate entry in the *Encyclopédie*, 'les passions et les intérêts des hommes font qu'ils s'opposent toujours au bien général lorsqu'il leur paraît contraire à leur intérêt particulier'?[12] The answer must be that no individual or group of individuals could ever aspire to square such a circle. It would be necessary to fall back upon some abstraction, some metaphysical construct, to conceal the inadequacies of *homo sapiens*. In Scotland Diderot's contemporary, Adam Ferguson, was able to argue confidently that the inequality between citizens contributed to the ready acceptance of the sovereignty of the state. In France, the mind of Jean-Jacques Rousseau was turning towards the concept of the General Will.

Rousseau was more concerned with the moral integrity of the individual than with the extent of his political freedom. He had no great faith in man's ability, including his own, to devise political relationships capable of satisfying each citizen's demand for liberty and equality. After reading his discussion of democracy in *The Social Contract*, with its despairing conclusion, 'Were there such a thing as a nation of Gods, it would be a democracy. So perfect a form of government is not suited to mere men', it becomes impossible to interpret the General Will as other than a harbinger of the abstract state.[13] It was a secular justification, that is to say, in the absence of divine right support, for a less than Utopian regime. Rousseau had already indicated his pessimistic view of the effects of social and political intercourse upon the human condition in his *Discours sur l'inégalité*. There he described how, with the coming of social organization, man lost his natural liberty and, with the acquisition of property, his natural equality too. For Rousseau, therefore, it was a matter of making the best of man's predicament as a social and political animal. He shared those humanitarian instincts which made the leaders of the French Enlightenment hostile to the various residual forms of serfdom. But he had few illusions about the difficulties involved in freeing humanity from the indignities of oppression and inequality. True equality he believed to be unattainable. He contented himself instead with the objective 'that power should need no sanction of violence but be exercised solely by virtue of rank and legality, while wealth should never be so great that a man can buy his neighbour, nor so lacking that a man is compelled to sell himself'.[14] As for the acquisition of liberty, that could only be rendered possible for Rousseau by endowing the political organization with a moral purpose. Thus man could acquire civil liberty by accepting the laws of the community. These were laws which through the exercise of the general will he had helped to frame, laws which justified the holding of property, laws therefore which countered the loss of liberty and equality inherent in society. In this way Rousseau reached the paradoxical position of asserting that liberty was in the gift of the general will and possessed validity and meaning only in its service.[15]

Though paradoxical, Rousseau's position was perfectly logical. He accepted that 'humanity's first law is that of self-preservation'.[16] *Ab initio*, therefore, the essential human drama concerned the desperate search for security rather than the struggle to be free. Because that quest demanded increasing subordination on the subjects' part it was necessary to distinguish between willing and involuntary servitude. This could be effected by investing voluntary submission with characteristics attractive to individual human beings. However, since such characteristics were fundamentally at odds with the overriding need for security, it was also necessary to resort to a fiction, to invent 'a legal person' through whom the contradictions could be resolved. Thus in the closing decades of the eighteenth century as the fatal inadequacies of the *ancien régime* were becoming clearer, the *Philosophes* added their blueprints for the future.

## ABBÉ SIEYÈS AND THE COMING OF THE REVOLUTION

The herald of the new order in France was the abbé Sieyès, who published his highly influential *Qu'est-ce que le tiers état?* some six months before the storming of the Bastille. In this work we find fully developed the idea of a society, a community, a nation, composed of individuals who each bear the same relationship to the government: 'a monarchy, like any other political system, requires only rulers and subjects'.[17] What it did not require and could not tolerate was privilege. Privileged groups could not be considered members of the community because they did not participate on an equal basis in that community by accepting common laws and a common order. Whereas under the *ancien régime* such privileged contractual arrangements with the ruler were the norm, they appeared now to be exceptional, as sovereignty shifted from the monarch to the people. But was the concept of sovereignty when thus asserted a more practical proposition than when applied to kings? Sieyès had some well-founded doubts on the matter, as he indicated by his remark that

> Sooner or later, every class will have to withdraw inside the boundaries of the social contract . . . Will this result in reaping its countless advantages, or in sacrificing them to despotism? . . . Will the changes we are about to experience be the bitter fruit of a civil war, disastrous in all respects for the three orders and profitable only to ministerial power?[18]

The only way to ward off such disconcerting questions was by facing them directly, in translating popular sovereignty into a political system beyond human accountability, immune to the fallibility of its servants.

Sieyès offers the most significant clue to his thinking in his comments upon international relations.

> We must conceive the nations of the world [he argues] as being like men living outside society or 'in a state of nature,' as it is called. The exercise of their will is free and independent of any civil form. Existing only within the natural order, their will can take full effect . . . its [the nation's] will is always the supreme law.[19]

In this way, by equating the state's right to survive with that of the individual in his pre-societal condition, Sieyès offers an amoral justification for state action which could not be extended to the individual citizens who had granted it sovereignty. Indeed by that very fact they submitted themselves to whatever laws were deemed necessary for the nation's security, at home and abroad. Political liberty, therefore, had perforce to follow meekly where state security led, an uncomfortable fact which Sieyès could not altogether disguise, even from himself, as he sought like so many after him, to stand the argument on its head. Though 'The law . . . protects what exists until what exists begins to be harmful to the common interest'; nevertheless, he maintains, 'These are the only limits set to personal freedom.' And again, 'all are equally dependent on the law, all present it with their liberty and their property to be protected; and this is what I call the common rights of citizens'. However, Sieyès does not always sound so sure. 'But let us not dissimulate,' he exclaims at one point, 'the guarantee of public liberty lies only where real power lies. We can be free only with the People and by the People.'[20]

One other aspect of Sieyès' thought deserves to be noted in the present context, his attitude to property. He strongly approved of Calonne's abortive scheme for the establishment of provincial assemblies, which would take into account not the personal status of the participants but their ranking as property owners. In this he typified the attitude of those who made the liberal revolution of 1789–92, whose views were quintessentially those stated in the *Declaration of the Rights of Man and Citizen*. These men were the owners of property, both noble and bourgeois, who, Professor Taylor has assured us, had sufficient in common in economic terms at least, to make them a single group.[21] For them the possession of property remained 'a sacred and inviolable right', one of the natural and inalienable rights of man. The architects of the Declaration were simply rewriting the old contract between the men of property and the sovereign, with the former, who now incorporated the whole political nation, also embracing the latter.

For these men liberty remained what the *Philosophes* had long proclaimed it to be: the power, as determined by law, to do whatever was not injurious to others. There was a vague shadow cast over their defence of the owners of property by the assertion that a 'legally established public necessity' might deprive them of it.[22] But this constituted scant preparation for the realities of 1793–94, the year of 'Virtue and Terror', when Maximilien Robespierre dominated the Committee of Public Safety. Under his direction a government dictatorship, forged in the people's name, silenced its critics by the guillotine. Thus those expectations of liberty with which the Revolution had begun were summarily snuffed out.

## SPAIN UNDER THE BOURBONS

In contrast to their French cousins the Spanish Bourbons presided over a thorough-going change of direction during the eighteenth century.

Unlike the old enemy, the Dutch Republic, Spain finally committed itself to the path of centralization and rejected the debilitating tradition of federalism. Like most political decisions, the new order was imposed in response to circumstances. In this case the circumstances were dramatic, those surrounding the demise of the royal Habsburg line and the succession of the French Bourbons. Philip V's coming to Madrid in 1700 has been compared with the arrival there almost two centuries before of the Burgundian Charles V.[23] It may be equally illuminating to compare the young French king's succession to the Spanish throne with that of his illustrious forbear, Henry IV, to the throne of France.

Both men inherited kingdoms so riven by internal divisions as to be threatened with dissolution. Both had to find ways of neutralizing dangerous centrifugal forces. Both were assisted by previous attempts in that direction. For although the rule of the Spanish Habsburgs ended ignominiously under the pathetic figure of Charles II, they and their predecessors had fought a number of successful battles from the end of the fifteenth century against the nobility, the towns and the Cortes.[24] Both too were able to build upon earlier foundations in a climate favourable to the imposition of firm royal authority. The Castilians rallied to Philip V's cause from the beginning of the War of the Spanish Succession. Their determination that the Bourbons should inherit the Spanish crown was strengthened by the fact that their traditional rivals, the Catalans, committed themselves to the Allied camp, which was associated with the Protestant cause and Portuguese and Imperialist interests. When in 1707 a son was born to the wife of Philip V, and the Franco-Castilian forces under the command of the Duke of Berwick won the victory of Almanza, Castilian resolve in favour of their Bourbon monarch hardened further. The result for Spain from this point in the eighteenth century was the growing identification of the personality of the sovereign with the state over which he ruled. The king's political authority, French-style, became increasingly unchallengeable. Eventually the time arrived when it was impossible to distinguish between the royal domains and the territorial boundaries of the Spanish state, between the aims of the ruling dynasty and those of the political community.[25] The country undoubtedly drew strength from this application of the Louis Quatorzian principle, however expressed, of 'L'état, c'est moi'. However, whether Spain was merely reinvigorated by a new and forceful dynasticism or was launched in actual fact upon the road to impersonal statehood, is a question requiring further examination.

The first point to be made is that the coming of the Bourbons to Spain brought no social revolution. The nobility remained the dominant order in the eighteenth century thanks to its extensive territorial possessions and its seigneurial rights. In 1800 the nobility and the church held over two-thirds of the land of Spain, with the former possessing almost three times the amount of the latter.[26] Secondly, it was certainly true that the new dynasty was primarily concerned with dynastic considerations. In May 1713 Philip V decided to modify the Spanish law of succession in order to prevent a female from succeeding to the throne unless there was no male heir in either the direct or the collateral line. This act could be interpreted as an attempt to guard the new-found authority of central government, particularly against foreign-born descendants – an ironic inference in view of Philip's French origins. But it should be seen primarily as an adaptation of the French Salic law which had successively secured the dynastic interests of the Capetians, Valois and Bourbons. It was Louis XIV himself who had suggested the measure in the first place.[27] The strength of royal absolutism in the eighteenth century was sufficiently assured for Spanish kings to revert to the practice of adopting their separate titles in respect to their individual possessions. Hence the style of King of Spain was replaced by that of King of Castile, of Leon, Aragon, Navarre, Granada, Toledo, Valencia and so on. Yet this eighteenth-century revival, with its separatist or quasi-federal overtones, did not signal any diminution of the unity of the Spanish kingdom. Rather it was a measure of self-proclaimed confidence in the authority of the Bourbon line. It was, too, a style practised by other contemporary absolutist rulers, such as Frederick II of Prussia.[28]

Philip V did not share the indifference of his Castilian subjects to the loss of the Spanish Netherlands and the Italian possessions at the Peace of Utrecht in 1713.[29] His foreign policy, especially after his marriage to the daughter of the duke of Parma, Isobel Farnese, in 1714, was geared to the task of restoring part at least of the lost Italian lands to the children of that second marriage, Don Carlos and Don Felipe. The means employed included two treaties with Bourbon France in 1733 and 1743, both of which contained a reference – significant language – to an irrevocable family pact.[30] Eventually Philip succeeded in establishing Don Carlos as king of Naples and Sicily and Don Felipe as duke of Parma and Piacenza.

Philip's involvement in these Italian adventures demonstrates a deep-rooted dynasticism which was resistant even to the painful memories of a disintegrating Spanish Habsburg empire. Not that Philip sought to recreate that empire. It seemed unlikely that Don Carlos would succeed in Spain; and when he did, as Charles III, he renounced his rights to the Italian kingdoms. Nevertheless, Philip's experiences in the early years of his kingship might have made him reflect on the disadvantages of extra-peninsular commitments and on the advantages accruing to him from their disappearance. The Spanish Habsburgs had been substantially weakened in their later years by the so-called 'Spanish system', the far-flung empire which was so difficult and expensive to defend. Franche-Comté had been lost to France in 1678, while the loss of Flanders and the Italian lands in 1713 reduced Spain's European possessions to a far more manageable and defensible shape.[31] Philip V and his advisers, including Frenchmen like Orry and Amelot, embarked upon a policy designed to strengthen further the power of central government at the expense of separatist peripheral forces within the peninsula. The first crucial decision was that taken in 1707, in the wake of Almanza, to abolish the ancient liberties, the *fueros*, of Valencia and Aragon. Henceforth, only the Castilian writ would run in these provinces: the long-standing system had begun to crumble. However, the most independent of all the Spanish regions, Catalonia, remained defiant even after being abandoned by the Allies in 1712, declaring war on Philip V in July of the following year. This particular Spanish civil war ended in September 1714 with the surrender of Barcelona. In January 1716 a new order, the *nueva planta*, was introduced which removed all the elements of separate Catalan identity. In the words of one of Catalonia's most distinguished historians, 'L'Etat catalan cesse d'exister.'[32] The gathering of royal power in Madrid was given provincial expression by the intendants whose office, originally instituted in 1711, was re-introduced by Fernando VI in 1749. Especially in organizing royal finance, they proved to be highly effective agents of the Crown.[33]

At this point we might pause to consider some of the implications behind these policies. Initially it appeared that the new dynasty's authority, based upon hereditary succession, would leave it as vulnerable as the old to local separatism. Philip V undertook in 1701 to 'confirm all the . . . cities, towns and villages in their immunities, exemptions, enfranchisements and privileges'.[34] What modified that characteristically dynastic arrangement were the circumstances surrounding the dynasty's establishment. For the first decade and a half of his reign Philip had to fight on Spanish soil, first a war for survival against foreign invaders, and then a civil war. One effect was to rally the Castilian people to his standard for Castile was fighting to retain its position as the power base of Spain.[35] In a restricted sense, therefore, the dynasty's authority depended upon national support. However, there were no mechanisms available to translate that support into an effective partnership. It fed on the pent-up frustrations aroused by present Castilian humiliations and by experiences in the preceding reign: monarchical incompetence, misgovernment, the pervading sense of impotence and decadence, and not least, the sympathetic stance adopted by Charles II and his entourage to Catalan particularism.[36] It could be expressed only in terms of encouraging the emergence of a regime strong enough to restore Castilian self-esteem.

The government was not slow to exploit its opportunity. In

abolishing the privileges of Aragon and Valencia in 1707 Philip V was emboldened to claim the power to re-write the law as he saw fit: 'one of the principal offices and rights that attach to Kingship is that of Law Giver, wherein are comprehended both the prerogative of creating new laws and that of rescinding old ones, and that We are accordingly empowered to alter the Statutes of the Realm as circumstances themselves do alter'.[37] This theme of unfettered absolutism was echoed in the writings of royal servants from Melchor de Macanaz, who claimed that all political rights and authority were granted by the Crown and could be reclaimed by it, and who implemented Philip's new order in Valencia and Aragon; to the count of Campomanes, a firm supporter of Charles III's enlightened absolutism.[38]

Against this centralist absolutist approach must be set the ultimately discredited Catalan alternative. The Catalans argued that they were fighting not simply for Catalonian separatism, as had been the case in 1640, but for the true interests of Spain, of which Catalonia formed a part. They contrasted the true liberty of a decentralized Spain with the stultifying oppression of Castilian-based absolutism. This attitude was much influenced by commercial considerations. Catalonia had enjoyed an economic revival in the late seventeenth century and the middle-class Catalan merchants favoured a political structure affording them maximum trading opportunity. Its capital, Barcelona, looked away from Spain towards the markets of the Mediterranean world and even further afield. The Dutch were their model, free traders who had broken away from Madrid over a century before rather than submit to its regulation and control. If the Catalans could not persuade the Spanish government now to adopt their point of view, then they too perforce must break with Madrid.[39] In the event, and leaving out of account the crucial geographical difference between Catalonia and the seven Dutch provinces in relation to Castile, they lacked the power to do so. For the force of Bourbon absolutism was proving irresistible, offering its own form of freedom. The loss of the Aragonese and Valencian *fueros* was depicted as the acquisition by all the king's subjects of identical rights:

> so that by this means my faithful subjects of Castile may obtain offices and employment in Aragon and Valencia, just as the Aragonese and Valencians may henceforward obtain them in Castile without any discrimination; so that I may thereby allow Castilians to enjoy further the marks of my gratitude in granting them the highest gifts and graces, so merited by their tested and proven loyalty, while giving to the Aragonese and Valencians similar and equally great proof of my clemency, by making them eligible for that which they were not eligible even amid the great liberty of the *fueros* which they used to enjoy . . .[40]

It appeared that 'centralisation is neither more nor less than liberty itself' was indeed to be the maxim for the future.[41]

The coming of the Bourbons to Spain, then, transformed the authority of dynastic kingship. With movement towards centralized government and towards political equality amongst the subjects, the ground was prepared for the emergence of the concept of the abstract state.[42] That it made no further headway before the French Revolution may be accounted for by the fact that Bourbon dynasticism was too deeply rooted to allow the family to take second place to an abstract ideal.

Thus the most successful and respected of Spanish Bourbon kings, Charles III, was able to preside over a regime of bureaucratic intervention and control without losing the universal personal regard in which his subjects held him. He expelled the Jesuit order from Spain in 1767, thereby clearing the way for state intervention in higher education. Henceforth university teachers and graduates were forbidden to teach ultramontane beliefs likely to challenge the secular power's authority over the church in Spain. Universities were subjected to political control and censorship, and curricula were devised for vocational studies likely to be beneficial to state service. Charles encouraged the study of natural and international law by making it compulsory for lawyers wishing to practise in Madrid, and by giving life-pensions to the most successful.[43] He sought to redistribute uncultivated land amongst landless peasants and provided government funds for the purchase of tools and livestock and to improve irrigation. He set up government-supported factories with a monopoly in their field, instituted technical education for the workers and decreed a range of crafts to be considered honourable and compatible with noble rank.[44]

Charles III and his officials set out to regulate the life of the Spanish community along lines which they judged best suited to serve the public interest. In other words they embarked tentatively upon the path leading to modern bureaucratic statehood. Yet Charles III was no *roi bureaucrate*. The government's power ultimately lay in the personal authority of the king. When he died in 1788 there were no signs of hostility to the monarchy, no feeling of imminent change. The acceptability of royal government sprang from the widespread admiration for the king's personal qualities, his religious devotion, conscientiousness, frugality, loyalty to the memory of a wife who had died within a year of his accession. It is worth noting that unlike France and England in the same period, Spain suffered few bread riots and was able to maintain the regime of free trade in grain which Charles introduced in 1765.[45] Even after his death and the outbreak of the French Revolution, the impact of his reign continued to be felt. News of the execution of Louis XVI was greeted with as much bitterness in Barcelona as it was in Madrid, proving that loyalty to the concept of personal kingship remained at a high level throughout Spain.[46]

It was not possible, of course, to shelter Spain indefinitely from the effects of the French Revolution. Charles III's trusted secretary of state who was re-appointed by his successor, Charles IV, the count of Floridablanca, did his best by introducing strict censorship and 'attempting to play a successful Canute to the tide of revolutionary publications'.[47] Eventually, however, Spain was caught up in the politics of the Revolution and of the Napoleonic empire, and the old patrimonial loyalty to the ruling dynasty began to lose its savour. The constitution drawn up by the Cortes in 1812 contained in its first chapter the significant phrase, 'The Spanish nation is free and independent and it is not nor can it ever be the property of any family or person.'[48]

The Bourbons of eighteenth-century Spain applied ideas of administrative kingship far in advance of those developed in *ancien régime* France. Whereas French kingship was inhibited by a long tradition of personal monarchy, the Spanish kings were actually assisted by the newly generated force of their dynasticism. This enabled them to exercise a power that came close to the despotism of the state but was rendered acceptable by the familiar royal forms in which it was expressed. Charles III was not the first servant of the state as his contemporary, Frederick the Great of Prussia, claimed to be. He combined that vision of service for the public good with an even greater dynastic sense than the Hohenzollerns possessed. That potent dynasticism gave him an authority unmatched among contemporary European rulers on both sides of the river Elbe.

## REFERENCES AND NOTES

1. W. Doyle, 'The Parlements of France and the breakdown of the old regime, 1771–1788', *French Historical Studies*, VI (1970), p. 431.

2. S. L. Kaplan, *Bread, Politics and Political Economy in the Reign of Louis XV*, 2 vols (The Hague 1976), II, p. 588.

3. See, for example, the comments of Roland E. Mousnier, *The Institutions of France under the Absolute Monarchy, 1598–1789* II: *The Organs of State and Society* (London 1984), p. 682, and Jean Egret, *Louis XV et l'opposition parlementaire* (Paris 1970), pp. 222–3.

4. J. F. Bosher, *French Finances, 1770–1795* (Cambridge 1970), *passim*.

5. *Ibid.*, p. 34.

6. Clive H. Church, *Revolution and Red Tape: the French ministerial bureaucracy, 1770–1850* (Oxford 1981), p. 45.

7. J. H. Stewart, *A Documentary Survey of the French Revolution* (New York 1951), p. 90. J. H. Shennan, 'The political vocabulary of the Parlement of Paris in the eighteenth century', *Atti del quarto congresso internazionale della società italiana di storia del diritto* (Florence 1982), II, p. 957, note 22.

8. Jean Egret, *La pré-révolution française, 1787–1788* (Paris 1962), p. 110.
9. *Ibid.*, p. 54, note 2.
10. M. Bordes, 'Les intendants éclairés de la fin de l'ancien régime', *Revue d'histoire économique et sociale*, XXXIX (1961), 57–75.
11. Denis Diderot, *Encyclopédie*, 17 vols (Neuchâtel 1765), vol. 15, p. 253: 'Société'.
12. *Ibid.*, vol. 15, p. 424: 'Souverains'. See too vol. 9, p. 472, 'Liberté civile'.
13. Jean-Jacques Rousseau, *The Social Contract*, translated by Gerard Hopkins for *Social Contract* (Oxford 1971), p. 233.
14. Rousseau, *The Social Contract*, p. 217.
15. *Ibid.*, pp. 104–6.
16. *Ibid.*, p. 170. *Discours sur l'origine et les fondements de l'inégalité parmi les hommes* (1755 Paris, 1973 edn.), p. 94.
17. Emmanuel Joseph Sieyès, *What is the Third Estate?*, trans. M. Blondel (London 1963), p. 178.
18. *Ibid.*, p. 96.
19. *Ibid.*, pp. 127–8. The idea had already been expressed by Rousseau in his *Discours sur l'origine et les fondements de l'inégalité parmi les hommes* of 1755, pp. 108–9.
20. Sieyès, *op. cit.*, pp. 95, 162.
21. George V. Taylor, 'Noncapitalist wealth and the origins of the French Revolution', *American Historical Review*, 72 (1967), 469–96.
22. Stewart, *op. cit.*, p. 115.
23 H. Kamen, *The War of Succession in Spain, 1700–15* (London 1969), p. 42.
24. G. Añes, *El antiguo regimen: los Borbones* (Madrid 1976), p. 300.
25. *Ibid.*, p. 297.
26. A. Dominguez Ortiz, *Sociedad y estado en el siglo XVIII español* (Madrid 1976), p. 351. Raymond Carr, *Spain, 1808–1939* (Oxford 1966), p. 39.
27. Añes, *op. cit.*, p. 302. G. Desdevises du Dézert, 'Les institutions de l'Espagne au XVIIIᵉ siècle', *Revue Hispanique*, 70 (1927), 1. A. Baudrillart, *Philippe V et la cour de France*, 5 vols (Paris 1890–1901), I, pp. 516–17.
28. Añes, *op. cit.*, p. 301. For Frederick the Great's titles, King in Prussia, Elector of Brandenburg, Duke of Pomerania, Prince of Halberstadt and Minden, Count of Mark and Ravensburg, etc., see Hans Rosenberg, *Bureaucracy, Aristocracy and Autocracy: the Prussian experience, 1660–1815* (Cambridge Mass. 1958), pp. 27–8.
29. Dominguez Ortiz, *op. cit.*, p. 36.
30. W. N. Hargreaves-Mawdsley (ed.), *Spain under the Bourbons, 1700–1833* (London 1973), pp. 98, 109.
31. R. A. Stradling, *Europe and the Decline of Spain* (London 1981), pp. 207–8.
32. P. Vilar, *La Catalogne dans l'Espagne moderne*, 3 vols (Paris 1962–64), I, p. 675.
33. Henry Kamen, 'El establecimiento de los Intendentes en la administracion española', *Hispania*, 95 (1964), 370–1.
34. Hargreaves-Mawdsley, *op. cit.*, p. 10.
35. Kamen, *The War of Succession in Spain*, pp. 218–19.

36. Dominguez Ortiz, *op. cit.*, p. 38. Vilar, *op. cit.*, I, p. 671.
37. Hargreaves-Mawdsley, *op. cit.*, p. 36.
38. H. Kamen, 'Melchor de Macanaz and the Foundations of Bourbon Power in Spain', *English Historical Review*, CCCXVII (1965), 712. C. C. Noel, 'Opposition to enlightened reforms in Spain: Campomanes and the Clergy, 1765–1775', *Societas*, III (1973), 24.
39. Vilar, *op. cit.*, I, p. 673. J. Vicens Vives, *Approaches to the History of Spain* (Berkeley, Calif. 1970 ed.), pp. 111–13.
40. Kamen, *The War of Succession in Spain*, pp. 302–3.
41. Carr, *op. cit.*, p. 64.
42. Vicens Vives, *op. cit.*, p. 116.
43. Richard Herr, *The Eighteenth-Century Revolution in Spain* (Princeton 1955), pp. 164 ff. Jean Sarrailh, *L'Espagne éclairée de la seconde moitié du XVIIIᵉ siècle* (Paris 1954), pp. 199 ff.
44. Herr, *op. cit.*, p. 126. W. J. Callahan, *Honor, Commerce and Industry in Eighteenth-Century Spain* (Harvard 1972), pp. 52–5. Laura Rodréguez, 'The Spanish riots of 1766', *Past and Present*, 59 (1973), 127–8, 144–5.
45. Herr, *op. cit.*, p. 310.
46. *Ibid.*, p. 258.
47. Hargreaves-Mawdsley, *op. cit.*, p. 238.

# Chapter five

# RUSSIA (I): MUSCOVY'S POLITICAL ORDER AND THE IMPACT OF PETER THE GREAT

## THE NATURE OF THE MUSCOVITE STATE

The history of Muscovy before the reign of Peter the Great is fundamentally different from that of any other state discussed in this work. Muscovy's political organization was of a most rudimentary kind, though its inchoate structure may serve to throw light upon those more advanced models which, during the eighteenth century, Russian rulers strove to emulate. Historical circumstances had allowed the Grand Dukes of Moscow to lead the Russian world out of the long period of Tartar domination which had begun in the early thirteenth century with the mass migration of Mongol tribes under the leadership of Genghis Khan. During the following century and a half the combination of a favoured geographical position and an initial policy by her rulers of cooperation with the new overlords enabled Moscow to emerge as the centre of native opposition to the invaders. After the Muscovites' first victory over the Tartars at Kulikovo (1380), the grand dukes of the house of Riurik gradually asserted their pre-eminent authority not only over their erstwhile masters but also over native rivals, such as Novgorod, Pskov, Tver and Ryazan'. Muscovite power was most clearly established during the three long consecutive reigns of Ivan III (1462–1505), Vasili III (1505–33) and Ivan IV (1533–84). The state which they gathered into their grasp, however, was essentially a private patrimony. There was no distinction between ownership and authority – the Roman concepts of *dominium* and *imperium* – for the primacy of Byzantine over Roman influences in the Russian lands was one of the most crucial of formative historical circumstances.[1]

The grand-dukes and their successors, the tsars, enforced a servitude upon all their subjects which was reinforced by the propoganda of an increasingly obscurantist orthodox church. There was no question of a social contract of the kind which in the West buttressed Bodin's concept of sovereignty. The population was divided into men of service and men of burden. The first were a tiny minority who possessed the land and serfs and who also carried out the rulers' military and administrative tasks, and the second were the vast majority, who paid taxes, worked the land and bore the physical load. But the former, though they enjoyed a quality of life superior to that of their unfortunate serfs, remained equally the chattels of the tsar, with no legal dispensation to shield them from the full force of his awesome authority. As late as 1805, the tsar's adviser, Michael Speransky, was still able to observe that there were but two estates in Russia, 'slaves of the sovereign, and slaves of the landlords'.[2] The men of service were categorized under such headings as *boyar, deti boyarskie, dvorianin*, untranslatable words since translation would inevitably and inappropriately suggest western-type concepts of gentry and greater and lesser nobility. For what no men of service could claim was absolute ownership of their land. All land belonged to the tsar, who merely leased it out in return for whatever services he required. There was thus no distinction between the tsar's public and private interests, nor between his subjects' public and private obligations. All relationships depended upon the ruler's pre-emptive disposition.

In a world of such amoeba-like simplicity there could be no collective bargaining for privilege. That would have implied an independence of status and therefore a degree of political sophistication beyond that possessed by the Muscovite model. Relationships, including those between the ruler and his most senior servants, were universally brutal: a fair indication of the political immaturity of the regime in comparison with contemporary western models. The matter was put succinctly by a seventeenth-century visitor to Muscovy, the German diplomat and scholar, Adam Olearius, who tells us that 'the Tsar, or Grand Prince, alone rules the whole country; all his subjects, the noblemen and princes as well as the common people, townsmen, and peasants, are his serfs and slaves, whom he treats as the master of the house does his servants'.[3] While great men who failed to appear at the tsar's public audiences were no longer beaten with the knout, but imprisoned instead, they remained in a literal sense captives in his patrimony. A Russian commentator, Grigori Kotoshikhin, who wrote several decades later that Olearius, confirmed that, 'If a prince, or a boyar, or anyone else, should go abroad . . . without informing and petitioning the tsar, he would be charged with treason, and his patrimonial estates and *pomest'ia* and possessions would be confiscated by the tsar.'[4]

Thus it becomes clear that the political regime under which Muscovy functioned before Peter the Great was at least one stage behind that of contemporary Western Europe. Political liberty had no meaning whatsoever, either in terms of individuals or of group 'liberties'. Equality on the other hand had a political meaning in Muscovy: it meant the total subjection of all the subjects to the personal dictates of the ruler. At this point a paradox may be observed. In the West possessory, patrimonial kingship implied a fundamental inequality between subjects, while the growth of administrative kingship tended towards equality of treatment. In Muscovy the situation seemed to be at least in part reversed. There patrimonial government produced a universal equality of servitude; it remains to be seen whether, in the eighteenth century, administrative, bureaucratic developments would stimulate the emergence of unequal relationships between tsar and people.

The paradox may be accounted for by the fact that we are not comparing like with like. There was a fundamental difference between the two concepts of royal office which is best illustrated by reference to the contrasting legal traditions. Whereas in the West the king's office was inherited along with a host of legal obligations which to a considerable extent prescribed its holder's authority, in Muscovy the tsardom offered the incumbent unrestricted power. There was a true paradox in this contrast, for whereas in the West the ruler's office itself inhibited the gratification of personal ambitions, in Muscovy it facilitated it. Whereas the power of French monarchs was based primarily upon a law of succession, that of the tsars depended upon the office itself, however acquired.

Therefore, the regime's insistence upon universal equality in the face of the single source of law and justice in the land – the tsar – should not be interpreted as indicative of an emerging state sovereignty. On the contrary, its highly personalized aura distinguishes it clearly from the impersonal despotism of the state. Nevertheless, it did provide some grounds for movement from the one towards the other, and during the seventeenth and eighteenth centuries efforts would be made in that direction. However, before examining that process in detail there is one special aspect of Muscovy's development which lies so close to the heart of this thesis that it deserves particular consideration: the cossack phenomenon.

## COSSACKS, SERFS AND THE STATE OF NATURE

The cossack appears to represent the antithesis of all those subjects, *sluzhilie liudi* – men of service – as well as serfs and slaves, who were governed by the Moscovite tsar. He stands for the adventurer, unwilling to be tied to the service of any state, a pre-Romantic child of nature epitomizing the individual's yearning for personal freedom. Though the reality was far more complicated than the myth, there is no denying that the cossack-serf dichotomy offers a powerful stimulus to the historical imagination: so powerful that we might easily over-look the fact that neither extreme alternative had a sustainable political future.

There are two ways in which we might explore the implications for our central theme of the cossacks' role. First, we may consider them as constituting a 'state of nature', that doomed stage of human association which, according to the constructs of seventeenth- and eighteenth-century political theorists, precedes the formation of political society. There are differences in interpretation between, for example, the views of Hobbes, Locke, Hume and Rousseau, but all share the assumption that men in the state of nature were free and equal. Hobbes' remark that 'Nature hath made men so equal, in the faculties of body, and mind' is precisely echoed by Hume: 'When we consider how nearly equal all men are in their bodily force, and even in their mental powers and faculties'. 'This equality of men by nature', in Locke's phrase, is put differently by Rousseau three-quarters of a century later: 'However strong a man, he is never strong enough to remain master always.'[5] The state of nature implied equality then and liberty too, the liberty to take whatever measures the individual felt were necessary to provide 'for the preservation of his own nature', until 'a point was reached in the history of mankind when the obstacles to continuing in a state of Nature were stronger than the forces which each individual could employ to the end of continuing in it'.[6] Only Locke differed fundamentally from these conclusions, suggesting in his *Second Treatise on Civil Government* that the 'ought' of moral responsibility was already present in the natural state, precisely because of the equality of man. For him, therefore, liberty was a communal attribute, a social rather than an individual characteristic.[7]

The origins of the Cossacks are obscure. Though mostly Russians, they were not exclusively so, for the derivation of 'cossack' is 'free man' or 'vagabond'.[8] The cossacks had no ethnic identity, therefore, but were defined by their lifestyle. They gathered from the mid-fifteenth century upon the south-eastern border of Muscovy, along the rivers Don, Iaik and Terek, and on the lower Dnieper in the south-west, where the Zaporozhian Cossacks had their island base. These warriors of the southern steppe formed a buffer between the Tartar tribesmen whose forbears had established Genghis Khan's great Mongol Empire, and the emerging states of Poland-Lithuania and Muscovy. During the sixteenth century serfdom was becoming the most prominent socio-economic feature in both these latter countries. There was no shortage of recruits, therefore, to the cossack bands as fleeing peasants sought refuge in the so-called 'wild country' of the wooded steppe.

What they entered might indeed be called a state of nature, with no obligations and no law save that of self-preservation. They were free to fight for their own survival and welfare, and initially they shared a political and economic equality. The basic instrument of cossack democracy was the Assembly, which every male had the right to attend. There the division of the community's spoils was agreed and hunting and fishing rights shared out on an equal basis. A rudimentary executive was necessary, of course, to implement the Assembly's decisions. But the *Ataman* was the Assembly's creature, not its master, and the failure to appreciate that fact proved fatal to a number of incumbents.[9]

What the cossack way of life most prominently lacked, however, was security. Cossacks were fighters and quite indifferent as to whom they fought – Turks or Tartars, Poles or Russians. In the absence of any external enemies they were content to fight amongst themselves. Indeed, Assembly meetings regularly concluded in blood-letting, and the *Ataman*'s authority frequently waxed or waned according to his physical prowess. In the state of nature therefore, for the Cossack, though explicitly not for John Locke, liberty meant licence. But were these cossack hosts in fact living in a state of nature? It must surely be admitted that in one sense they were not, for at the moment when each individual, refugee or adventurer or criminal, joined a cossack band he entered society. One is reminded of the fact that the concept of the social contract contained two related ideas, the idea of a contract of society and that of a contract of government.[10] They are not ideas to be easily separated and the assumption must be that the establishment of a society presages the way in which that society will be governed. That was particularly so with Thomas Hobbes, who argued that men, finding the prospect of perennial warfare in the state of nature thoroughly undesirable, sought peace and security by entering a civil society of such a kind as to produce those ends. He states his position clearly in *De Cive*:

> Since therefore the conspiring of many wills to the same end doth not suffice to preserve peace, and to make a lasting defence, it is requisite that, in those necessary matters which concern peace and self-defence, there be but one will of all men. But this cannot be done, unless every man will so subject his will to some other one, to wit, either man or council, that whatsoever his will is in those things which are necessary to the common peace, it be received for the wills of all men in general, and of every one in particular.[11]

Yet that was palpably not the situation in which the early cossack hosts found themselves. Their state was much closer to nature than to a civil polity. Their society was no more than the individual expression writ large of a personal freedom which could only be articulated and maintained in war. Hobbes' own definition of the bellicose natural state fits the cossack communities well enough: 'the nature of war, consisteth not in actual fighting; but in the known disposition thereto, during all the time there is no assurance to the contrary'.[12]

69

The practical example provided by the Cossacks seems, therefore, to cast doubt upon the validity of theoretical analyses which hinge upon that distinction between two contracts, one social and one political, so favoured by writers of the Social Contract school. Hobbes' exposition is not the only one to leave the Cossacks uncomfortably situated in a state of limbo if not of nature. Jean-Jacques Rousseau also posited a two-stage development from the state of nature to one of mature civil government, the first a social pact, the second a political one which gave universal recognition to the General Will. However, as with Hobbes the two contracts were not separable, the latter being already implicit in the former. In Rousseau's words, 'there is no way in which they [men] can maintain themselves save by coming together and pooling their strength in a way that will enable them to withstand any resistance exerted upon them from without. They must develop some sort of central direction and learn to act in concert.'[13] On a very superficial level the cossack communities under their ataman leaders might be seen as fulfilling this definition of social and political organization, but the reality was different. Their *raison d'être* was not to guarantee peace but to make war, to exercise power by coercion, not by moral suasion. And Rousseau did not recognize in the exercise of such power the expression of legitimate political authority:

> If I am waylaid by a footpad at the corner of a wood, I am constrained by force to give him my purse. But if I can manage to keep it from him, is it my duty to hand it over? His pistol is also a symbol of Power. It must, then, be admitted that Might does not create Right, and that no man is under an obligation to obey any but the legitimate powers of the State.[14]

John Locke's state of nature was already a society with laws which entitled its members to act in defence of life, liberty, health and possessions. The political contract merely marked the transition to a more sophisticated regime in which, rather than taking the law into their own hands, the citizens agreed to establish an executive authority to enforce that law in their name.[15] The state of permanent instability and insecurity which cossackdom represented on the southern and western frontiers of Muscovy during the sixteenth and early seventeenth centuries, reflected neither the political sophistication of Locke's civil society nor the commonsensical civility which characterized his state of nature.

David Hume came closest to matching the theory to the reality. For him the original agreement to subordinate the self to a social grouping, at the same time accepting membership of a political order, was no more than a starting point. The pact allowed a charismatic leader to exercise some brief authority, the particular needs of the moment dictating a particular response. Gradually as such responses became habitual, something approaching a permanent compact replaced the earlier *ad hoc* relationships. Thus political society progressed to the point at which the power of fleets and armies guaranteed to the contracting parties that security and freedom which their own natural forces could never have commanded.[16] Once more we are reminded of the eighteenth-century concern with progress, though Hume remains perversely independent in assessing its direction. Not for him an emphasis upon the citizens' right of resistance to an unworthy sovereign who fails to keep his promises; but instead an ironic recognition of the growing power of government to enforce its decrees willy-nilly upon the subjects:

> Were you to preach in most parts of the world, that political connexions are founded altogether on voluntary consent or a mutual promise, the magistrate would soon imprison you as seditious for loosening the ties of obedience; if your friends did not before shut you up as delirious, for advancing such absurdities.[17]

Hume's compatriot, Adam Ferguson, avoided the difficulties surrounding the concept of the state of nature by denying that the idea had any validity at all. Instead he concentrated on the continuum of man's social-political development over countless generations, starting from the assumption that man's natural state is to live in society. That society would become progressively more complex and mature, until ultimately – and in this Ferguson reflected the new anthropological history of his century – it would decay and disappear.[18] His approach, and Hume's, suggest a second way in which to explore the cossack phenomenon and its relationship with the Russian world.

## COSSACKS AND THE STATE OF MUSCOVY

It is possible to view cossackdom and the Muscovite state of the sixteenth and seventeenth centuries as standing for opposite political extremes. Each was a threat to the other and neither was capable of permanent survival. They represented a thesis and antithesis which had to be reconciled if the Russian state was to evolve unscathed in the increasingly dangerous world of international European politics. The freedom of the Cossacks was for the Russian authorities mere anarchy, the absence of government; whereas for the Cossacks Muscovy under the tsars was a regime of slavery, characterized at every level by the absence of freedom. Did not the tsar's very title of *gosudar'* proclaim him to be lord over slaves? Yet between these diametrically opposed forces of Cossacks and tsar there were connecting links.

Chiefly they were united by a shared sense of insecurity. That was the essence of cossack existence, while Muscovy had to face the threat of Turks and Tartars to the south, and more powerful sophisticated enemies to the west. The overriding needs of Russian security made it impossible for Moscow to leave the Cossacks free to add their own anarchic threat to her frontiers. The initial, successful alternative was to employ the cossack hosts as paid frontier guards. Gradually the Muscovite government tightened its control over these mercenaries, who came increasingly to depend upon the military and economic support provided by the tsar. A Don Cossack petition of 1659 to Tsar Alexis (1645–76), father of Peter the Great, makes that fact abundantly clear: 'Deprived of your bounty, Sire, deprived of provisions, we, your slaves, are perishing; . . . and lacking gunpowder, Sire, and lacking lead, we are delivered to your enemies.'[19] Eventually the various hosts were all forced into submission. The Zaporozhian Cossacks of the Ukraine accepted union with Moscow in 1654, and inexorably thereafter cossack freedoms were restricted, usually in the wake of unsuccessful revolts against the government. Thus after the Bulavin rising of 1707–8 the Don Cossacks lost their independence and saw their region incorporated into the province of Voronezh. The effect of the Pugachev revolt on Catherine II some sixty-five years later was traumatic enough to persuade her to instigate a policy which has also proved popular with her Soviet successors. She pronounced 'the very name of Zaporozhian Cossacks abolished for all time to come', while the Iaik Cossacks, who had strongly supported Pugachev, were renamed the Ural Cossacks as a means of eradicating memories of that most serious of all the peasants upheavals in *ancien régime* Russia.[20]

Long before the eighteenth century, however, less dramatic influences coming down from Moscow and Warsaw had begun to change the face of cossackdom. In the Ukrainian borderlands between the two rival states of Muscovy and Poland-Lithuania the latter continued to hold the upper hand until the second half of the seventeenth century. As the Polish gentry edged their way into the rich grain-producing land of the Ukraine, enserfing the local population, it became necessary to deal with the cossack problem. Ignoring the Zaporozhians' armed and well-nigh impregnable camp beyond the cataracts of the lower Dnieper, the Poles concentrated on the less fiercely independent Cossacks to the north and west. First, from the early sixteenth century they were 'registered' as permanent military employees of the Polish crown. But that was simply the thin end of a wedge which the Polish authorities sought to drive deep into the social fabric of the region. Favoured cossack leaders received land and status. A propertied cossack elite began to emerge and some even became Polish noblemen. With a stake in the land and status and privilege to protect, these Cossacks were willingly absorbed into a political order which, though it deprived them of their traditional free lifestyle, gave them security. For security loomed large when economic and social inequalities became significant.[21] Thus the opposed extremes of cossack and serf were reconciled in a one-sided fashion, a recognition of the fact that the nature and extent of liberty had to be defined in terms of order and stability, and not vice-versa. To the east the Don Cossacks were gradually divided between the established 'householders' who monopolized the region's richest hunting and fishing areas and received grain and money from the tsar; and the so-called 'naked ones', more recent, destitute refugees, the followers of Stenka Razin who led the great Cossack revolt of the late 1660s. Razin promised to restore the old cossack ideals of freedom and equality and for several years the region between the Don and the Caspian Sea returned to something approaching that natural state in which life was nasty, brutish and short. On this occasion at least, it was a well-documented condition. Significantly, the revolt ended when Don Cossacks loyal to the tsar captured Stenka Razin and handed him over to Moscow for execution.[22]

A still more intangible influence pulled the Cossacks towards the tsar: religion. Particularly after the foundation of the Uniate Church in the Ukraine (1595) which recognized the supremacy of Rome and gained the landowners' allegiance, the Ukrainian Cossacks identified with the rival Orthodox church which held the loyalty of the poor peasants. Since the fall of Constantinople to Islam in 1453, Moscow had claimed to be the custodian of the one true faith, the Third Rome, and that posture exercised a powerful influence on the cossack hosts. Yet it was to the Orthodox tsar rather than to his Muscovite kingdom that the Cossacks expressed their allegiance. A distinction grew in the seventeenth century between the Russian state, representing a servile regime which was anathema to the cossack spirit, and Holy Russia, representing all Orthodox believers within and outside the frontiers of Muscovy.[23] It was possible in the eyes of the Cossacks to revere the tsar as the standard-bearer of the true faith without submitting to his secular regime. Nevertheless, such a strong ideological pull could only assist the ruler of Muscovy in the task of consolidating his authority in the frontier regions.

## THE INFLUENCE OF HOLY RUSSIA

It is now time to consider further the nature of tsarist authority in the century before Peter the Great. We have already noted that the office of tsar did not acquire its legitimacy from legal succession as French kingship did. Indeed, it is easier to identify such negative distinctions than to categorize positively the source of that authority. Certainly the power of the grand dukes had been nurtured by the conquest of neighbouring Russian city states. In theoretical terms, however, their authority appeared to come directly from God in a unique fashion. The principles of secular government entered the Russian world in the wake of Christianity, so that the ruling prince was and continued to be perceived first and foremost as a champion of the faith. When a member of the grand-ducal family suffered what in the West would have appeared to be political assassination, he became a martyr in Holy Russia. The *ex-officio* sanctity of his life set him apart from other men and contributed to the myth of a succession of saintly princes.

The problem with such authority was that it could be falsely claimed by pretenders whose credentials could not be readily checked. Consequently Russian writers were faced with the difficult task of distinguishing between legitimate and illegitimate tsars. Their arguments tended to be circular: legitimate action depended on the legitimacy of the ruler which in turn could be established by reference to those actions.[24] What was not difficult to demonstrate was the irresistible personal power of the tsar, any tsar, once he had acquired the office.

However, that power was not of a kind to come to terms with the sophisticated political ways of western Europe which, during the second half of the seventeenth century, were beginning to impinge on the Russian consciousness. Particularly after 1667 when the treaty of Andrusovo gave the Russians Kiev and a foothold on the right bank of the Dnieper, western influences from Poland flooded into Moscow. That same treaty heralded Muscovy's emergence from the shadow of Polish-Lithuanian domination, as a European power of some consequence with an interest in opposing the Swedes in the north and the Turks in the south, as well as keeping a watchful eye on the old Polish adversary to the west. Yet the autocratic authority of the tsar, who at this time was the 'Christ-loving, pious, God-crowned, most gentle prince Aleksei Mikhailovich', was ill-suited for such an international role. The epithets before his name reinforce the extraordinary nature of Tsar Alexis's task. His primary obligation was to preserve inviolate the unique Russian Orthodox faith. Surrounded by heretics and infidels, he was both the guardian and the prisoner of the Third Rome. His every public act was a religious ceremony. Whereas Louis XIV's progress through his kingdom could be charted by the royal palaces at which he stayed – Versailles, Fontainebleau, Marly, Vincennes – Alexis's travels were from one monastery to another.[25] Although all his subjects were equally his servants, his power over them was off-set by the curiously negative nature of his function. His fundamental task was to maintain the status quo as the doctrine of the Third Rome required. For if Holy Russia were to fall into error as its two predecessors – Rome itself and Constantinople – had done, tsardom would be undermined and with it the integrity of the Muscovite state.

Yet the reign of Tsar Alexis did witness one significant conflict which was crucially to affect the future relationship between the secular and spiritual powers. The Patriarch Nikon, the spiritual head of the Russian church, introduced a number of reforms in 1653. These were intended to bring the Russian church back into line with original Greek Orthodox practices. The decrees offended many of the traditionalists in the church and led to a major schism, the Great *Raskol*. Subsequently Nikon claimed that the spiritual authority had ultimately to take precedence over the temporal power. Alexis resisted this claim and Nikon was removed from the patriarchate. Thereafter a weakened church found itself increasingly dependent upon the support of the tsar and vulnerable to attack should the ruler choose to kick over the traditional traces.

During the seventeenth century such an eventuality seemed unlikely. For the nature of tsarist authority continued to inhibit the development of secular government machinery capable of harnessing that power and directing it into politically effective channels. The difficulty was compounded by the abiding absence from Muscovy of any Roman law influences. Written law had never been important in a country where the proclaiming of justice and truth – and the two concepts were inseparable – could be infallibly entrusted to the pious voice of the tsar.[26] The fact that his voice was frequently and palpably lacking in piety and in any other Christian virtue, as in the case of Ivan the Terrible, in no way diminished the powerful myth which gave the tsar his authority.

In the time between the accession of Peter I and the death of Catherine II, however, with which the following sections will be concerned, an attempt was made to modify the nature of Russian government by recourse to law and regulation. Efforts were made to utilize the enormous reserves of central government power to activate and then regulate and control the political nation. Such a regulatory regime had few roots in Holy Russia, though it would be misleading to suggest that changes only began to take place in the reign of Peter the Great. Important Muscovite law codes had been promulgated in 1497 and 1550 by Ivan III and his grandson, Ivan IV, respectively. There was also the great Council code, the *Sobornoe Ulozhenie* of 1649, issued by Tsar Alexis. A Soviet historian has recently made the point that the *Ulozhenie* provides the first full legal account of the movement towards absolutism, of the extension of government control over central and local affairs and over the church.[27] Nevertheless the scale of activity quickened significantly with the reign of Peter the Great, justifying a narrower focus on eighteenth-century Russia.

## THE IMPACT OF PETER THE GREAT

It is in fact perfectly proper to describe Peter I as a revolutionary, as a man committed to a radical refashioning of the state along lines quite alien to the Russian tradition. His efforts were destined to fail as surely as Joseph II's one-man revolution would later fail to transform the Habsburg empire. Exactly a century after Peter's death the Decembrist conspirators too would fall as ineluctably before the autocratic force of established dogma. The fact is, of course, that the body politic treats imported ideas as suspiciously as the human body does transplanted organs. Peter inherited a regime in which the most uncompromising autocratic power was complemented by the subjects' universal deference, according to the precepts of the Russian Orthodox church. There were no corporate rights or traditions of the kind which in the West had resulted in a series of contracts between government and governed. Nor was there a legal tradition adequate to sustain such contracts. The most striking parallel in western eyes between the regimes of the tsar and the sultan was 'the neglect of legal norms in public administration, carried on by predominantly irresponsible and corrupt functionaries'.[28] In a state where the leading figures, the nearest equivalent to the noble class in the West, were known as 'serving men' and were content to describe themselves as slaves to the tsar, the concept of political freedom was irrelevant.

Peter intended to modernize the Russian state, not by introducing his subjects to western-style liberties, but by capitalizing upon the tradition of slavish acquiescence to the authority of the tsar in order to construct an impersonal state-machine. His early years coincided with a time of crisis for Muscovy. The schism of the Old Believers and the struggle between Patriarch Nikon and Peter's father, Tsar Alexis, over the relative rights of church and state, threatened to undermine old values. Cultural cross-currents ebbed and flowed in Moscow, following the acquisition in 1667 of Kiev and the Polish Ukraine. The resulting sense of unease and uncertainty was reflected in Peter's own upbringing and in the ambiguity of his own outlook. None of his predecessors had evinced the curiosity in Europe west of the Dnieper which Peter demonstrated in the Great Embassy of 1697–98. Yet Peter remained the most patriotic of tsars, determined to employ whatever concepts and techniques the West might provide simply to further his country's power and security.

It is a truism to observe that military and naval strength lay at the heart of Peter's designs. During the seventeenth century the Russian army had been growing more professional. Peter's reforms were designed to produce a fully professional force, nurtured by new government adminstrative routines which the military reorganization had called forth. This was the system, if that word does not too greatly overstate the degree of coherence involved, through which Peter sought to effect his revolution. He appeared to believe sincerely that an all-powerful, regulatory state would be a universal blessing for his subjects. In the words of one recent commentator,

'For him, "the common weal" and "the good of the state" were identical ideas'.[29] That Peter could reach such a conclusion owes something to his acquaintance with West European political thought with its emerging concept of reason of state. Also, the theory of Thomas Hobbes offered powerful support to the principle of unlimited royal power matched by the subjects' absolute submission, and Peter's most influential adviser, Archbishop Feofan Prokopovich, made much use of it in his own political writing.[30] Yet the tsar was also beholden to his native tradition which bestowed such a plenitude of power upon the holder of the tsarist office. How well does Hobbes' metaphorical language accord with the Muscovite doctrine:

> As in the presence of the master, the servants are equal, and without any honour at all; so are the subjects, in the presence of the sovereign. And though they shine, some more, some less, when they are out of his sight; yet in his presence, they shine no more than the stars in presence of the sun.[31]

It is not difficult to comprehend therefore how Peter the Great could envisage transforming Muscovy into a modern state, capable of holding its own against its European rivals. The commitment of all the subjects to that primary obligation became their essential function, guided by the sovereign's supreme duty to the same cause.[32] To carry out this transformation, however, it would be necessary to replace the ideology of the Third Rome with a secular ethos and to give to the written law a significance that it had not previously acquired in the Russian world.

The dismantling of the Third Rome was completed in 1721 with the establishment of the Most Holy All-Ruling Synod in place of the Patriarchate. This process of secularization was primarily the work of Peter himself.[33] Henceforward the Russian church would no longer be the guide and inspiration of the temporal power but merely a cog in the state machine. The tsar's chief obligation would no longer be expressed in the essentially passive terms of the defence of Holy Russia. Instead, he became the chief executive of a secular power, responsible for the regulation and control of mechanisms intended to maintain for that power a despotic authority over the subjects comparable to tsardom's former lordship over slaves.

Russian and Soviet historians have long debated the questions of Peter's debt to the West for his administrative reforms, and of whether his borrowing was crudely unmodified or adjusted to take account of Russian conditions.[34] Behind this debate lies the still more significant question of the nature of Peter's vision of the state. According to one of the most distinguished of Peter's biographers, M. M. Bogoslovskii, his ideal was the Western European state governed by an absolute prince committed to the pursuit of the common good and guided by the dictates of reason. This was to be a state in which widely recognized legal regulations would replace the arbitrary government of old Moscovy.[35] But where, one must ask, in the Europe of Peter's day was such an ideal translated into practice? Certainly the doctrine of monarchical absolutism, the exercise of political authority restricted only by the law, was a commonplace. But the cameralist implications which Bogoslovskii rightly identifies as characteristic of the Petrine approach appear anachronistic. Even Sweden, which most commentators agree furnished the compelling model for Peter to follow, was an unconvincing exemplar. For although it is true that from the 1680s Charles XI's *reduktion* policy had greatly strengthened the power of central government in Sweden at the expense of the great nobility, that power still depended upon its quasi-contractual links with the noble estate. And although inter-necine warfare between the magnates and the gentry in Sweden at first assisted the king's drive towards absolutism, its ultimate effect, paradoxically, was not the elimination of opposition to an all-powerful state but the reiteration by a unified noble estate of the constitutional balance between the Crown and its most privileged subjects.[36]

Peter's inheritance was quite different. The power of the Grand Prince and later the Tsar of Muscovy had no 'contractual' implication whatsoever. It reduced all the subjects to the same subservient level. By simply replacing the religious with a secular justification for that relationship Peter did indeed anticipate eighteenth-century develop-ments in state absolutism. The absence from the Muscovite theocracy of any limiting obligations further encouraged the emergence of the idea of impersonal state power. For it is worth repeating that it was not the legal inheritance of the office of tsardom that bestowed authority but the office itself, however acquired. A strong dynastic tradition tended to inhibit the rise of the state-idea. Peter, on the contrary, was indifferent to that tradition, and, having connived at the death of his only son, Alexis, he went so far as to assert the right to choose his own successor. In the event he failed to do so. His second wife, a woman of undistinguished peasant stock, succeeded him as Catherine I. But in the long run Peter left his country at the mercy of noble factions.[37]

Was Peter the Great able therefore to effect a revolution in gov-ernment and society on the basis of his country's singular inability to fit the absolutist models of his western rivals? Such a leap-frogging concept could scarcely succeed for very long, though the de-termination and vision of one man achieved remarkable short-term results. From the end of 1717 Peter established his central gov-ernment colleges and local government agencies on the Swedish model, attempting to regulate and regularize the administration of justice, commerce and industry, and the armed forces. Earlier, in

1711, he had created the Senate and later, in 1721, as we have seen, he established the Holy Synod.

However, in the face of a hostile Russian tradition the regime which he planned never became a reality. The great mass of official decrees issued during his reign were never codified nor did the written procedures required to establish the law's validity ever oust the tsar's spoken commands. The law remained an aspect of his power, unchecked by administrative procedures.[38] Hence the Holy Synod found that it could do nothing without Peter's approval and had to submit to his regular intervention and interference.[39] Equally, the ruling Senate, which liked to remind its ecclesiastical rival, the Synod, of its overall authority in civil affairs, regularly found itself by-passed by Peter's unilateral decrees and browbeaten by favourites like Menshikov and Apraksin.[40] In Petrine Russia, where government structures were indeed becoming more complex, power was obscured rather than curtailed by the application of the law. In this respect the Russian situation threatened to produce a caricature of the British model where sovereignty was genuinely buried in the political machine.

But Peter's failure to establish a regime based on the concept of the abstract state was most apparent in his relationship with those who, following his own example, were expected to serve it. Since the Muscovite serving man possessed no corporate rights to set against the demands of central government, like those tacitly acknowledged in Versailles between the Crown and the noble estate, there should have been no question of a mutually acceptable arrangement. Peter's vision was of one-way obligation inspired not by a belated desire to govern in harness with the landowning class but in the tradition of lordship and service characteristic of the Russian *gosudarstvo*. For whereas in the West the status of nobleman imposed an obligation in honour to serve the prince, in Russia it was upon that service to the tsar or the grand-duke that status depended.[41] The ancient system of *mestnichestvo* abolished in the year of Peter's accession in 1682, had for more than two centuries ranked the status of the various leading families in Muscovy according to the distinction of their service. The term is derived from the Russian word for a place, *mesto*. It was an elaborate genealogical system designed to ensure that successive generations of service families retained their status relative to each other. This was accomplished by rules enforcing an unchanging hierarchy based upon positions previously held. The drawbacks of such a system, both for the government's freedom of action and for the recruitment of new, dynamic elements among the service class, are obvious. Similarly, the Table of Ranks, established by Peter the Great in 1722, re-affirmed the principle that social status depended exclusively on the degree of commitment to the regime.

However, attitudes amongst the proto-noble class were beginning to change. During the seventeenth century provincial serving men were establishing independent economic bases, becoming regional gentry with a stake in the land. Meanwhile the great metropolitan families began to accumulate large estates and take on the appearance of a Western European aristocracy.[42] The process of integration of the serving man into a privileged noble class was taking place and the abolition of the *mestnichestvo* was a sign of that development.[43] Such a process had serious implications for the autocracy since it implied a *quid pro quo* relationship based on mutual dependence. The nobility's service might ultimately be given only in return for economic, social and even political privileges. Already in the 1680s Prince Golitsyn, the close adviser of Peter's powerful half-sister, the Regent Sophia, had proposed that the tsar should be joined by a twelve-strong consultative body of boyars which would assist, and no doubt restrain, the autocrat in the exercise of his authority.[44]

Once more we are confronted by the dichotomy of liberty versus authority and once more the question of security is to be found at the heart of the issue. For the freedoms which the embryonic noble estate were seeking in the seventeenth century could scarcely have been contemplated if the government had not established a more secure regime. From 1613, during the first decades of Romanov rule, the inadequacy of the Muscovite serving men against Swedish and Polish forces led to the recruitment of the so-called 'new model forces'. These consisted chiefly of foreign officers and Russian peasant infantry troops. The new formations proved far more effective than the cavalry formations of the old service gentry. By the 1680s there were some 80,000 troops of the new kind under arms and only about one military serving man in five was required for active service.[45] The question then arose of what was to happen to the estates – *pomest'ia* – held in return for state service that was no longer needed. The logical response would have been that they should be returned to the tsar who needed all the resources at his disposal to pay for the new improved military machine. Indeed, Golitsyn drew up such a plan during the 1680s, based upon the contemporary *Reduktion* by Charles XI of Sweden. It would have involved the loss by serving men of *pomest'e* estates and of the serfs who maintained them. It failed because moves towards the emergence of an integrated noble class were too powerful to be reversed. The *Ulozhenie* of 1649 had tied the serfs in perpetuity to their owners and given legal backing to the transformation of service land into hereditary estates. The ownership of land and of serfs was becoming a monopoly of the nobility and the church.[46] Though in the short-term, therefore, the service gentry may have become superfluous soldiers, their determination to maintain the social and economic advantages attached to the possession of land and serfs would ultimately force the tsardom to negotiate terms with them. After the trauma of Peter's reign the Russian state machine went into reverse and that governing contract between the noble estate and the Crown, which had preceded the emergence of absolutism in the West, followed it in Russia.

However, it must not be assumed that Peter's reforms were uniformly detrimental to the interests of the nobility. His reign saw the further weakening of the distinction between service estates and land hereditarily acquired. In particular, the decree of March 1714 confirmed that 'All immoveable property, such as patrimonies and *pomest'ia*, whether inherited, obtained by service, or bought . . . shall not be sold or mortgaged but shall be retained in the family.'[47] In addition, the very proliferation of legal pronouncements encouraged the expectation that rights would become as clearly defined as obligations. Finally, the power of lord over peasant was increased in the course of Peter's reign. Peter's prime need was for money to sustain his massive war effort. To raise it he had recourse to a variety of expedients but the poll tax of 1718 had the most far-ranging social effect. For tax-paying purposes the population was divided into those who were liable to the tax and those who were not. Thus the category of bondman disappeared, translated to the status of serf in order to increase the number of those eligible to pay taxes. Russia was being pressed into a rudimentary division, in the words of Peter's most recent English biographer, M.S. Anderson, 'between a great peasant majority, largely unfree, which paid the new impost and a privileged ruling minority of landowners who did not'.[48] Such a division was necessary not only to fund the tsar's ambitious military and naval operations but also to enable his serving men to carry out the various obligations, civil and military, which he imposed upon them. They therefore acquired a superior legal status entitling them to own serfs, whilst the peasantry sank to the level of a 'mass resource', to be exploited as the needs of the state required.[49]

Why was it the case then that Peter's service state was not warmly welcomed by its servitors? Answers to that question can only be given after the subject has been examined on several levels. The tsar's military commitments and the administrative substructure needed to support them, had transformed an introspective theocracy into a power to be reckoned with in Eastern and Northern Europe, and one to be carefully weighed in the balance of West European diplomacy. Such a transformation called for the re-integration into state service of many of those who earlier had not had to be actively involved. This highly regulated regime of near permanent service threatened the improving lifestyle of the landed aristocracy. For many the result of this unwelcome recall to the colours was economic disaster, and numbers of gentry opted out of their obligations to become *odnodvortsy* (an in-between social category liable to the poll tax but entitled to own serfs), or even peasants.[50] Peter's plans were also rebuffed for a less tangible reason. His church reforms had brought the Third Rome down to earth, subjected it to the same sort of regulations and controls as the Senate and all the other institutions of government: indeed, the Ecclesiastical Regulation of 1721, which established the Holy Synod, itself refers pointedly to the tsar's military reorganization as an example to be followed.[51] The result was to deprive the tsardom of that aura which had previously justified the exercise of autocratic power. In place of the *tishaishii* tsar, clothed in the raiment of the last true faith on earth, stood an all-demanding autocrat who offered nothing to his servants save the obligation to serve: 'A partnership in which one party held all the power and played by its own rules.'[52]

## REFERENCES AND NOTES

1. Richard Pipes, *Russia under the Old Regime* (London 1977 edn), pp. 64–6.
2. *Ibid.*, p. 105.
3. A. G. Cross (ed.) *Russia under Western Eyes, 1517–1825* (London 1971), p. 99.
4. G. Vernadsky *et al.* (eds), *A Source Book for Russian History from Early Times to 1917*, 3 vols (London 1972), I, p.229.
5. Thomas Hobbes, *Leviathan*, Scolar Press Facsimile of the London 1651 edn (Menston 1969), p. 60. David Hume, *Of the Original Contract*, p. 148. John Locke, *Second Treatise on Civil Government*, p. 4. Jean-Jacques Rousseau, *The Social Contract*, p. 172. The works of Hume, Locke and Rousseau have been published (and in Rousseau's case translated) under the title of *Social Contract* (Oxford 1971), with an introduction by Sir Ernest Barker.
6. Hobbes, *Leviathan*, p. 64. Rousseau, *Social Contract*, p. 179.
7. Locke, *Second Treatise on Civil Government*, pp. 4–11.
8. See the comments by Terence Armstrong in the introduction to his edition of *Yermak's Campaign in Siberia*, The Hakluyt Society (London 1975), pp. 9–10.
9. Philip Longworth, *The Cossacks* (London 1969), pp. 35 ff.
10. E. Barker, *Social Contract*, p. xii.
11. Hobbes, *De Cive* (New York 1949 edn), pp. 66–7.
12. Hobbes, *Leviathan*, p. 62.
13. Rousseau, *The Social Contract*, p. 179.
14. *Ibid.*, p. 173.
15. Locke, *Second Treatise on Civil Government*, pp. 74–6.
16. Hume, *Of the Original Contract*, p. 149.
17. *Ibid.*, p. 151.
18. Adam Ferguson, *Essay on the History of Civil Society*, ed. Duncan Forbes (Edinburgh 1966), Part I, Section I, p. 4; *Principles of Moral and Political Science*, 2 vols (Hildersheim 1975), vol. I, pp 268–9.
19. Vernadsky, *op. cit.*, I, p. 279.
20. *Ibid.*, II, p. 459.

21. Longworth, *op. cit.*, pp. 90–2. Perry Anderson, *Lineages of the Absolutist State* (London 1974), p. 209. Even within seventeenth-century Muscovy itself so-called *kabala* peasants were voluntarily contracting themselves into a lifetime of service, usually as a *quid pro quo* for financial assistance; while the practice of entering into voluntary slavery appealed even to some high-born Russians anxious for security. Vernadsky, *op. cit.*, I, pp. 241–2. Jerome Blum, *Lord and Peasant in Russia from the Ninth to the Nineteenth Century*, Atheneum edn (New York 1964), p. 274.

22. Longworth, *op. cit.*, pp. 124–52.

23. Michael Cherniavsky, *Tsar and People* (New York 1961), pp. 112–14.

24. *Ibid.*, pp. 53–6.

25. *Ibid.*, p. 63.

26. Oswald P. Backus, 'Muscovite legal thought, the law of theft, and the problem of centralization, 1497–1589', *Essays in Russian History*, ed. A. D. Ferguson and A. Levin (Hamden 1964), p. 40.

27. A. G. Man'kov, *Ulozhenie 1649 goda* (Leningrad 1980), p. 257. Note, too, the comments of James Cracraft, *The Church Reforms of Peter the Great* (London 1971), p. 101, on the importance of the *Ulozhenie* as a source of precedents for state control over the church.

28. J. L. H. Keep, 'The Muscovite elite and the approach to pluralism', *Slavonic and East European Review*, 48 (1970), 205.

29. I. A. Fedosov, 'Sotsial 'naya sushchnost' i evolyutsiya rossiyskogo absolyutizma', *Voprosy Istorii*, 7 (1971), 56.

30. M. S. Anderson, *Peter the Great* (London 1978), p. 110. Cracraft, *op. cit.*, pp. 2, 49–62. There is no evidence that Peter himself was widely read. He preferred to acquire his ideas from conversations, especially with Prokopovich.

31. Hobbes, *Leviathan*, p. 93.

32. Fedosov, *op. cit.*, pp. 56–7. Peter's own sense of commitment is revealed in a stern letter to his ill-fated son, Alexis, p. 57, note 25: 'I did not and do not spare my life on behalf of my fatherland and people: how then can I spare you.'

33. Cracraft, *op. cit.*, p. 235.

34. The debate is summed up by Claes Peterson, *Peter the Great's Administrative and Judicial Reforms* (Stockholm 1979), pp. 11 ff.

35. M. M. Bogoslovskii, *Oblastnaya reforma Petra velikogo* (Moscow 1902), p. 24.

36. See below, pp. 111–12.

37. Anderson, *Peter the Great*, p. 156.

38. Peterson, *op. cit.*, pp. 331–2.

39. Cracraft, *op. cit.*, pp. 195 ff.

40. Vernadsky, *op. cit.*, II, p. 336. G. L. Yaney, *The Systematization of Russian Government: social development in the domestic administration of Imperial Russia, 1711–1905* (Urbana 1973), p. 65.

41. Marc Raeff, *The Origins of the Russian Intelligentsia: the eighteenth-century nobility* (New York 1966), pp. 19 ff.

42. Keep, *op. cit.*, 216 ff.

43. Peterson, *op. cit.*, p. 52. Raeff, *Russian Intelligentsia*, p. 28.

44. Keep, *op. cit*, 229.

45. *Ibid.*, 211. Peterson, *op. cit.*, p. 46.

46. Peterson, *op. cit.*, pp. 47 ff.
47. Vernadsky, *op. cit.*, II, p. 351.
48. Anderson, *Peter the Great*, p. 97.
48. Yaney, *op. cit.*, p. 132.
50. Raeff, *Russian Intelligentsia*, p. 60. Thomas Esper, 'The Odnodvortsy and the Russian nobility', *Slavonic and East European Review*, 45 (1967), 124 ff.
51. Cracraft, *op. cit.*, p. 263.
52. Pipes, *op. cit.*, p. 129.

# Chapter six

# RUSSIA (II): THE EMERGENCE OF THE NOBILITY

## THE GROWTH OF POLITICAL INDEPENDENCE

With the end of the awe-inspiring regime of Peter the Great resistance grew to the one-sided relationship between the tsar and his servants. His two immediate successors were ineffectual rulers. Catherine I (1725–27), Peter's second wife, was incompetent and under the dominating influence of her late husband's favourite, Prince Menshikov. She was succeeded by Peter's grandson, Peter II (1727–30) who was only twelve at the time of his accession. During these two reigns the Supreme Privy Council, composed of high-ranking court aristocrats, emerged as the most powerful central government body, It was this body which offered the crown in 1730 to Peter the Great's niece, Anna Ivanovna, together with the famous list of *konditsii* which she had to accept before becoming tsarina. These included her acceptance of the Supreme Privy Council's veto over matters of war and peace, the imposition of new taxes and promotion to high office in the civil, military or court hierarchy.

The support of the service class at large helped Anna to repudiate her promises and re-establish an autocratic regime. Historians no longer believe that the crisis of 1730 marked the failure of a genuine constitutional experiment in Russia. The threat of oligarchic rule was real enough to persuade most nobles that the stability and security imposed by the autocracy was preferable to the revival of factious struggles like those between the great rival houses of the Miloslavskii and the Naryshkin who had intrigued for power during Peter I's minority. Besides, the internecine rivalries amongst the high nobility left some of them more optimistic of obtaining preferment under a renewed autocracy than under a Privy Council dominated by their opponents.[1] Yet there was more to it than that. The form in which the conditions were set out was that of a legal contract. For the first time tsardom had been forced, however briefly, to acknowledge a set of rules which was not of its own devising. Although these rules were primarily intended to protect the interests of the Supreme Privy Council, they also sought legal safeguards for the gentry at large who were not to be deprived of 'life, possessions, or honor without [due proceedings in] a court of law'.[2] Efforts to establish a new social and political relationship between the tsardom and its chief domestic allies went back at least to Golitsyn's still-born scheme of the 1680s, and the crisis of 1730 widened the possibilities.

For although there was little support for the specific proposals of the Supreme Privy Council, the episode did provoke a significant debate among the nobility. Some of the petitions, like the final decisive document submitted in the name of Prince Trubetskoy, merely requested the restoration of the Petrine system. That petition, of 25 February 1730, provided the opportunity for the new Empress to reject, with the maximum dramatic effect, the conditions imposed upon her earlier.[3] But others were more ambitious and implied a quasi-independent role for the nobility in the maintenance of the common weal. The so-called project of the generals, for example, envisaged a large noble assembly, 'for important matters concerning the administration or the general weal of the state'. This was not an exclusively military petition but was drawn up by members of the top four ranks of the Table of Ranks, from the civil and court, as well as the military hierarchy.[4] Its signatories included high aristocratic names like Dolgorukii and Matiushkin, the latter a cousin of Peter the Great. The project relating to the rank-and-file nobility referred obscurely to a Diet (significantly the Russian word was borrowed from the Polish 'seym') which would devise whatever was necessary for the reform and welfare of the state, and submit its proposals for confirmation by the nobility. Prince Cherkasskii's petition alluded to the need to establish 'a safe system of government for the peace and welfare of the state in accordance with the opinion of the majority'.[5]

Though Anna quickly succeeded in re-establishing the authority of her office, the tide was beginning to run strongly in favour of a partnership between the tsardom and an increasingly self-conscious privileged class, an emerging second estate. The events following the death of Peter the Great had deprived the tsardom of some of its assurance in dealing with its chief servitors. In the thirty years following Anna's accession, the noble class succeeded in wringing major concessions out of the government. The controversial law requiring single inheritance, introduced by Peter I in 1714, was revoked in 1730. It had been a thoroughly unpopular measure, overturning as it did the long-standing Muscovite practice of dividing land equally amongst all the sons. The service obligation for children of the gentry to register at school was waived in favour of instruction at home. Twenty-five years became the maximum period of military service for the gentry and each landowner was entitled to keep back one of his sons to supervise the estate in his absence, on condition that he provided an alternative recruit instead. The state did not abolish compulsory service over these years, nor did the service class demand abolition. But it was becoming impossible for the government to enforce all its regulations in this sphere, however threatening the form in which they were drafted.[6] The problem for the emerging Russian nobility, whose status had always depended upon fulfilling its obligations to the government, was to discover an alternative justification to permit it to maintain a privileged place in society. It is at this point that the issue of political liberty first comes to the fore in the Russian context.

## THE EFFECTS OF EDUCATION AND THE ENLIGHTENMENT

The final emergence of the Russian nobility as a distinctive estate of the realm was aided by two closely related eighteenth-century developments. The first was its acquisition at one level or another of a formal education. Peter I had required young Russian noblemen to learn to read and write as a preliminary to undertaking state service. From that modest beginning the upper ranks of the nobility began to acquire a degree of cultivation and sophistication which set them apart from their peasants and also for a time from their less affluent provincial counterparts. The Empress Anna's Cadet Corps, founded in 1731, was indicative of the kind of education thought suitable for the small group of elite noble children, the future leaders of their estate. The dominating characteristic of its curriculum was the interest in Western Europe. Foreign languages, especially French and German, were studied there, as well as Western literature, elements of which were translated into Russian in the Cadet School. Gradually, in Marc Raeff's phrase, the outward manifestations of Western civilization 'filtered down even to the estate in the remote provinces'.[7] The effect was to give the nobility a sense of corporate identity as the natural leaders of society, beyond that bestowed by their role as chief servants of the state. The idea of a third element joined to the ancient duality of the autocracy and its servants was novel. The Russian words for 'social' and 'society' – *obshchestvennyi* and *obshchestvo* – only came into use during the second half of the eighteenth century, the former first penned by the distinguished historian and *littérateur*, Nikolai Karamzin.[8] The concept of society as an entity existing independently of the state, enabled the nobility as its natural representatives, to exploit the idea of an unwritten contract between themselves and the tsar, on the lines of earlier West European models.

Education exposed the Russian nobility to the stimulus of enlightened thought, though the doctrines coming into Russia from the West, German, French and British amongst others, by no means added up to a coherent programme. Aspects of the German *Aufklärung* and of the French and Scottish Enlightenments were eclectically acquired. Precepts of natural law entered from Germany, in particular with the works of Christian Wolf. Invariably the philosophers of the *Aufklärung* stressed the moral and ethical aspects of political relationships, and their emphasis upon progress and reason was set in a framework of communal rather than individual action. From France came Montesquieu's reflections on the law and its role as guarantor of collective rights, a work much studied and admired by no less a personage than the Empress Catherine II herself. Voltaire encouraged a fashionable scepticism towards religion and clergymen, especially in St Petersburg, an attitude made easier to adopt in the wake of Peter the Great's secularization of Russian society. Later in the century Rousseau's educational ideas were absorbed along with those of John Locke, quickening the belief in the possibility of self-improvement which could in turn change the face of society. This idea of progress was also the inspiration of eighteenth-century historians and they too were read. Karamzin looked to Gibbon and Robertson among contemporaries, while his intellectual rival, Alexander Radishchev, knew the works of Voltaire and Condorcet.[9] Both men were familiar with the politico-economic doctrines of the Scottish Enlightenment, though the sophisticated structures and relationships elaborated by Ferguson and Adam Smith were far removed from the realities of the Russian polity.[10] A good deal closer were the fierce criticisms levelled by the fiery French *abbé* Raynal against the system of serfdom.

The educated Russian nobleman thus imbibed a veritable pot-pourri of Western ideas which yet, paradoxically, fostered amongst them a sense of identity and common purpose. These ideas offered new foundations on which the noble might base his relationship with his serfs and with the tsar, new moral principles to replace those previously enunciated by the discredited Third Rome, new opportunities to make a name, not simply for himself and for his peers, but also for his country now that it was launched upon the path to enlightenment.[11]

There was, however, a problem. All these heady ideas had been nurtured in an environment vastly different from that of Russia. The simple 'contractual' relationship between government and property-owners that was gaining strength in Russia during the eighteenth century had already been weakened in the West, and it was precisely that decline which had permitted the expression of new ideas. Since there was no synchronization between the two areas, there was no way of telling what responses Russians might make to these western stimuli.[12] One of their first historians was Prince

Michael Shcherbatov (1733–90). He was an ardent supporter of Montesquieu and adopted the French philosopher's elevated view of the nobility's political role. He was familiar with the literature, history and philosophy of the Western Enlightenment, adopting its central tenet of rational enquiry as the means to discover the universal rules governing social and political behaviour. Yet his own background, Russian and orthodox, inevitably coloured his perceptions. In surveying his country 'with the eye of a man brought up on strict ancestral rules', he found the institution of serfdom entirely defensible, but the inner effects of westernization deeply disturbing:

> if, after entering later than other nations upon the path of enlightenment, nothing more remained for us than to follow prudently in the steps of nations previously enlightened, then indeed, in sociability and in various other things, it may be said that we have made wonderful progress and have taken gigantic steps to correct our outward appearances. But at the same time, with much greater speed, we have hastened to corrupt our morals.[13]

The political themes which underlay the Enlightenment in the West were the themes which this essay set out to explore: the nature of the subjects' liberty and of the power of central government. In the West the growth of the abstract authority of the state threatened to emerge as a concomitant of the subjects' equality in their relationship to government. In Russia the opposite tendency was becoming apparent. The debate in the West was taking place within a framework of complex and sophisticated political organizations, and that very complexity and sophistication made answers to the profound questions being posed, difficult to arrive at. Not so in Russia, where a more rudimentary form of government and social organization appeared to offer the perfect opportunity for clear choices to be made between the claims of individual liberty and government control. It will be necessary to return later to that debate. Before that, however, there is another factor assisting the emergence of the Russian nobility as a separate estate in addition to its educational advances and the influences of the Enlightenment which we must consider: the establishment of professional armed forces and of a bureaucracy capable of providing security without the assistance of large segments of the noble class.

## THE GROWTH OF A PROFESSIONAL MILITARY AND CIVIL SERVICE

The emergence of the Muscovite serving class had originally been prompted by the pre-eminent needs of security. By the mid-eighteenth century, following Peter the Great's introduction of the Table of Ranks, the signs were that both the armed forces and the civil service were once more recruiting adequate numbers of professionally minded noblemen to maintain a well-ordered and secure regime.[14]

Peter's establishment of the Table of Ranks had marked an important stage not only in his drive to recruit effective servants for the state but also in his recognition of noble, as opposed to service, status. The legislation of January 1722 set up three promotional ladders for government service, one military, one civil and one for the court. Those who reached the eighth rank automatically acquired noble status if they were not already noblemen.[15] It was the tsar's intention that the Table of Ranks should open the door to talent, and to some limited extent that aim was borne out in practice. However, the non-nobles who rose to such dizzy heights during the eighteenth century remained a small minority. The Table of Ranks also encouraged the growth of specialization and professionalism. This was especially true in the military sphere. There was thus no longer any need to call out all 50,000 of Russia's noblemen to keep the state secure, as had been the case in the 1680s, and the extraordinary pressures of Peter the Great's reign had likewise diminished.

However, the Table of Ranks had not changed noble attitudes fundamentally. Most continued to accept that service to the state constituted their only honourable vocation. Others with less elevated ideals simply could not afford to forego the income which rewarded such service. Even the less respected civil service was not to be discounted: in 1763 its salaries were substantially increased.[16] The government too assumed that service would continue to be the norm, even after emancipation. The Manifesto granting freedom to the nobility issued in February 1762 by the ill-fated Peter III spoke scathingly of 'all those who have never served anywhere, who pass all their time in sloth and fail to instruct their children in the arts and sciences beneficial to their country'.[17] The tsar's readiness to release the nobility by issuing this unprecedented legal enactment appears to have been prompted by two related motives: the need to reduce military expenditure at the end of the Seven Years' War and the desire to encourage those professional elements amongst the nobility who were committed to military or civil careers.[18] Freedom for the serving class from its obligation to serve meant an increase, not a reduction, in efficiency and therefore in state authority and control. But what was the meaning of liberty for those impoverished noblemen who were pleased to be free of their onerous burden of service, but who without it had no role at all? In the words of the provincial nobility of Pskov, submitted in 1767 to Catherine II's Legislative Commission,

The Russian nobility has only the freedom not to serve, and that alone, but having neither the resources nor the power for anything else, they live on their estates with a few poor possessions and many dependents; and even if someone wants to work at something that would be useful to the fatherland, his capability and his inclination are constrained to perish for want of means on the one hand and for want of permission on the other.[19]

## CATHERINE II's INSTRUCTION TO THE LEGISLATIVE COMMISSION

One of the problems confronting Peter III's successor, his wife Catherine II, was that of deciding whether to confirm the emancipation granted by her late husband. There were several difficulties involved. Assuming that the overwhelming ethos of the nobility remained one of service, what justification could there be for privileged treatment of those who were no longer required for service? One privilege which they certainly expected to retain was that of owning serfs. Indeed, the provincial nobility was intent on obtaining a legal guarantee of the exclusive right of noblemen to possess serfs, and to be free from state interference in their relations with them.[20] These were matters about which the Empress had reservations. As an intelligent German princess who had spent much of her childhood at the brilliant court of Brunswick-Wolfenbüttel, she enjoyed the intellectual stimulus of the European Enlightenment. Her ultimate acceptance of the fact that noble freedom would have to depend upon the enserfment of a large proportion of the Russian population was based upon pragmatism, not on intellectual conviction. Besides, she had no wish to see the nobility's freedom of action increased at the expense of the state's, which would certainly be the case if so many subjects were removed from its control. At the same time Catherine was mindful of the danger to her own position if she provoked the nobility beyond endurance on this issue. As an admirer of Montesquieu, she also recognized the feeling among the nobility at large that it was the compulsory nature of service, not the idea of service itself, which had offended the nobles' sense of honour and provoked so many demands for emancipation.[21] In the light of such conflicting and complex responses it is not surprising that Catherine had still not announced her policy on freedom for the nobility by 1767, when she published in Moscow her famous *Nakaz*, the Instruction to the Legislative Commission.

Catherine's decision of December 1766 to summon such a Commission was an interesting one. There was an evident need to codify the laws in the aftermath of Peter the Great's frenetic legislative activity. It is less clear why the tsarina should convoke such a large public assembly as the vehicle for this codification. Though not a representative body in the western sense, the Commission did bring to the capital deputies from a wide range of government and territorial groups. It seems that Catherine calculated that her authority would grow in the spotlight provided for her by the Commission. Though four and a half years had passed since she had seized the throne from her husband, Peter III, she had yet to convince the nobility at large that she had their interests at heart.

Catherine's Instruction, 'one of the most remarkable political treatises ever compiled and published by a reigning sovereign in modern times', was issued to coincide with the opening of the Commission at the end of July 1767.[22] An examination of this extraordinary document reveals something of the constraints under which Catherine was working. But more significantly for our purpose, it demonstrates how the injection into the Russian world of complicated arguments about political liberty and authority borrowed from the Enlightenment serves to illuminate some of the political realities of East and West.

The Empress was not yet prepared to accept the contractual bonds which western nobilities had earlier achieved with governments. She was however ready to acknowledge that a legal framework should govern her relationship with all the classes of society; and that the nobility could lay claim to particular rights: 'The Diversity of Rank, Family, and Condition established in a Monarchical Government, frequently gives rise to many distinctions in the Nature of Property, And Laws established upon the Constitution of this State increase still further the Number of these Distinctions.' And again, 'In all Governments where there are distinctions of Persons, there are necessarily Privileges confirmed to them by the Constitution.'[23] That was as far, however, as she found it possible to go. Despite quotations, direct or indirect, from Montesquieu and Beccaria, Diderot and d'Alembert, Catherine's *Nakaz* remained in essence a defence of state power against the various liberties to which her subjects aspired.

She tackled the question of liberty head-on in the fifth chapter of her Instruction: 'It is necessary to have a clear and distinct Idea what Liberty is.' She proceeded to offer not her own definition but Montesquieu's: 'Liberty is the right of doing whatever is permitted by the Laws,' and 'Civil Liberty is a Tranquillity of Mind arising from the Opinion that every individual of the whole Society enjoys his personal Security.'[24] But what did such high-sounding phrases amount to in Catherine's Russia. Did they imply more than the resolution of the old cossack-serf dichotomy by a sovereign power defined by its ability to impose its own definition of liberty on both parties? And were definitions of sovereignty and liberty fundamentally different in the wider western world where cossacks and serfs were scarcely to be seen? Cardinal Richelieu would certainly have approved of clause 136 of the Empress's Instruction:

But if the Legislative Power thinks itself in danger from secret conspiracy against the State, or the Sovereign, or from Collusion with Foreigners, in such Case, it may authorize the executive power to arrest persons upon Suspicion for a time, who only suffer a temporal Loss of their Liberty, in order to preserve it uninjured for ever.[25]

Several more of Catherine's glosses on Montesquieu's original version further illustrate the political realities which she identified behind the president's spirited defence of the monarchical state. She repeated a part of his argument in Book 2 Chapter IV of *De l'esprit des lois* on the subject of 'The intermediate Powers subject to and dependent upon the Supreme Power'. But she did not go on, as Montesquieu had done, to invoke the nobility as the intermediate power *par excellence*. Instead, she cited the government bureaucracy, the Senate, the Colleges and the inferior tribunals, making it clear in various clauses of the *Nakaz* that the country's judiciary was ultimately the sovereign's agent given a thin veneer of independence by the establishment of formal legal procedures. Though Catherine envisaged a government based on unspecified 'fundamental laws', she left her readers in no doubt that 'the Sovereign, who represents and holds in his own hands all Power for the defence of the whole Community' would always have the last word. Near the beginning of her Instruction, in clause 9, she stated unequivocally that 'The Sovereign is absolute, for no other than absolute Powers vested in one Person, can be suitable to the Extent of so Vast an Empire,' a thought-provoking observation in the light of Montesquieu's equally firmly expressed view that large Empires had to be governed despotically.[26]

As for the object of this absolute rule, it was not to procure the citizens' liberty but their glory together with that of the state and sovereign. What precisely that meant remains debatable both in the case of Catherine's Russia and of Montesquieu's France – for this too is a direct quotation from *De l'esprit des lois*. It was, however – Montesquieu again – an acceptable alternative to liberty: 'This Glory in a People under monarchical Government creates a Sense of Liberty, which in such States, is capable of producing as many great Actions, and of contributing as much to the happiness of the Subjects, as Liberty itself.'[27] From the moment of her accession Catherine had set out to establish her identitiy as the champion of official nationalism in the spirit of the great Peter, to restore to Russia the international reputation which it had enjoyed in his day, since when it had become the victim of foreign exploitation.[28] She much preferred, therefore, in 1767, to annex to this cause the French philosopher's rather ambiguous support than to confront the issue of liberty where it most starkly presented itself: in the matter of serfdom.

We know from other sources that Catherine was no supporter of the serf system, but she knew that the stability of the regime required her to keep her opinions carefully censored.[29] In the untitled eleventh chapter of her *Nakaz*, therefore, in which she skirted around the dangerous subject, she contented herself with quoting Montesquieu once again, this time in a phrase borrowed from the first book of *De l'esprit des lois*: 'that Government is most conformable to Nature, the peculiar genius of which corresponds best with the Genius of the People for whom it is established'.[30] The original maxim, which occurs in Montesquieu's introduction concerning laws in general, had no direct bearing upon the problem of serfdom. However, it provided Catherine with an enlightened formula behind which she could maintain the status quo.

## THE EFFECTS OF THE *PUGACHEVSHCHINA*: THE LAWS OF 1775 AND 1785

It is an ironic fact that in her efforts to consolidate the power of the state along lines first elaborated by Peter the Great, Catherine II should have sought the moral support of a philosopher, Montesquieu, who was totally hostile to the Petrine concept. However, the view from St Petersburg began to change dramatically from September 1773 when a Don Cossack called Emilion Pugachev proclaimed himself to be the dead tsar, Peter III, and raised a variety of discontented frontiersmen in revolt against the government.

The rebellion began amongst the Iaik Cossacks and spread rapidly. Pugachev was joined by a force of Bashkirs from the Ural region to the north which was the Russian government's heavy industrial centre. Mines and foundries were attacked and ransacked for arms and ammunition, and numbers of the state peasants who had been conscripted to provide an industrial labour force joined the rebels. Before the revolt ended, almost exactly a year after it began, Pugachev's motley army, numbering up to 20,000 men, had terrorized the steppe region between the rivers Don and Yaik and seriously alarmed the government. The capture of Kazan on the middle Volga fleetingly raised the spectre of a march on Moscow itself.[31]

The profound effect of the *Pugachevshchina* upon Russia's ruling classes may be judged not merely by the subsequent decrees of Catherine's government but by the long-lasting, residual fear in government circles that widespread peasant revolt would ultimately undermine the old order. The military threat posed by Pugachev in the short term was serious enough but the real danger lay in his invocation of cossack ideals of freedom which threatened a bloody rejection of serfdom from below. Pugachev's unrealistic programme envisaged a return to nature, as serfs became cossacks and a regime of licence rather than liberty swept away the powers of government and landowner alike. In his so-called manifesto of July 1774 Pugachev declared that all who were formerly peasants and subjected to landowners would receive

> freedom and liberty and the eternal rights of Cossacks, including freedom from recruiting levies, the soul tax, and other monetary taxes; we confer likewise the ownership of lands, forests, hayfields, fisheries, and salt lakes without purchase or rent; and we free the peasants and all the people from the taxes and oppression formerly imposed by the villainous nobles.[32]

The revolt was to provide the provincial nobility, who had lost their direct service obligation following Peter III's emancipation of 1762, with a new role which would justify the privileges to which they aspired. The *Pugachevshchina* also persuaded the Empress to prevaricate no longer over the issue of noble freedoms. In the interest of security she proceeded to work out a contractual arrangement which would satisfy both parties, government and nobles, and remove the threat of anarchy. The two legal documents which proclaimed the new deal were the Statute for the Administration of the All-Russian Empire of 1775 and a decade later the Charter of the Nobility. It would be quite wrong to suggest that these laws introduced an obligarchic regime, any more than Montesquieu's *De l'esprit des lois* had favoured noble domination. The tsardom remained in command of the situation, but at a price that was now legally recognized for the first time. That price was the maintenance of a socio-economic infrastructure which inevitably weakened the central government's freedom of action. Catherine acknowledged that the government bureaucracy could not hope to secure the vast extent of her Empire from the centre: she needed provincial agents to assist her.

The nub of the provincial reform statute was the reorganization of the Empire into smaller, more manageable administrative divisions which had the effect of doubling the number of provinces in Catherine's Russia. The provincial sub-divisions or districts increased threefold. At both provincial and district level, class courts were established for nobles, townsmen and free peasants, an indication of the new emphasis upon corporate rights and obligations which was replacing the Petrine ideal of universal service. The expansion of the provincial bureaucracy required many more officials than had previously been interested to make themselves available. Catherine's solution was to introduce the principle of election, again on a class (or estate) basis. The nobility were to elect ten members to their provincial court from among their own number, and the two members of their district court likewise. Similar arrangements were made for the burghers and free peasants. The important matter of policing the countryside, including the pursuit of fugitive serfs, was tackled by the establishment at district level of lower land courts, consisting of a land commissar and two assistants, all three elected by the district nobility. Finally, the nobles of each district were empowered to elect triennially a marshal who was charged with organizing the noble assembly which was responsible for the various elections. This assembly was given the right to submit collective petitions to the tsarina, a procedure calling to mind the *cahiers* of the second estate in France, drawn up at bailiwick level before meetings of the Estates- General. The author of the latest and most definitive biography of Catherine and her reign comments on the unusualness of such a right in Russia.[33]

In summary, therefore, the nobility as a class felt that the government in St Petersburg had at last signalled its need for an alliance, and their future as serf-owners in particular, appeared secure. Additionally, many individual noblemen benefitted financially from the establishment of so many new provincial offices, all of them paid for by the state.

Between the promulgation of the Statute for the Administration of the Provinces and the Charter of the Nobility Catherine became increasingly sympathetic to ideas of noble class consciousness and distinctiveness. In this she was much influenced by one of her governor-generals, Sievers of Novgorod, who himself appeared to be a disciple of the English constitution. He wrote of the alliance between the state and men of property in the pursuit of the common interest. He praised the responsible use of liberty, though he was referring, of course, not to the liberty of all the subjects but to the liberties of a particular group. Catherine responded with a decree of November 1778 which 'established the assembly of the nobility as an institution, transforming a congregation of nobles gathered together to do the bidding of the state into a corporate body'.[34] It only remained to spell out in full the legal identity of the noble estate.

The Charter of the Nobility was published in April 1785.[35] It confirmed for all time to come what it called 'the freedom and liberty of the honourable Russian nobility'. That did not mean that henceforth the nobles were freed from their age-old service obligation: rather that the rules of the contract between them and the government were clearly set out for the first time. There is no better example than the Charter of the relative weakness of personal government when the legal basis of its authority has to be publicly elaborated. Catherine's and Peter's predecessors, that line of priestly grand dukes and tsars, wielded an authority rendered awesome by the impenetrability of its nature, just as the mystery of divine-right kingship in the West shielded monarchs from too many probing questions. The pattern of political development in early modern Europe suggests that impersonal state power, which gave unprecedented authority to the central government, developed more readily in countries where sovereignty was veiled. Peter the Great had tried to capitalize upon Muscovy's obscurantist Third Rome tradition to establish a modern Russian state. The failure of that initiative was sealed by the publication of the Charter of the Nobility which, by the very openness of its legal pronouncements, exposed government and governed to the defence of an increasingly unsatisfactory status quo. This was the negation of that idea of progress which in a state like Britain, where sovereignty lay concealed within the complex and fluid definition of the king-in-Parliament, offered limitless opportunities for improvement.

By the terms of the Charter the status of noble was confirmed as hereditary. He had the right to trial by his peers. He was not to be subject to corporal punishment. He could travel abroad (and even enter the service of foreign allies). He was obliged neither to pay personal taxation nor to billet soldiers in his own home. He became a private landowner, finally freed from the old *pomest'e* obligation to repay landownership with service. He was also entitled to buy villages. This last clause (number 26) is the closest that the Charter comes to the issue of serfdom, for the purchase of villages presumably included the villagers who lived and worked there. Madariaga makes the point strongly that the Charter did not in any formal sense increase the power of the nobility over their serfs: 'It simply left the existing situation unchanged.'[36] However, in the light of Catherine's outlook towards the end of her reign, it seems reasonable to interpret the omission of any legal pronouncement on serfdom as evidence of the government's willingness, in so far as the rights of the serfs were concerned, to allow its writ to run no further than the entrance of the lords' estates. The nobility also acquired certain corporate rights. Their assembly in each province was empowered to make representations to the governor on matters affecting its corporate needs and welfare, and ultimately to the Senate and the tsarina.

The *quid pro quo* required by the government in return for these concessions was the continued support of the noble class against threats from within and without to the autocratic tsarist regime. Article 20 of the Charter reiterated the nobility's ultimate obligation:

> But since the honourable title and dignity of a noble shall in the future be acquired, just as it was in times past and is today, by service and efforts beneficial to the empire and the throne and since the essential condition of the Russian nobility depends upon the security of the fatherland and the throne, therefore at any time needful for the Russian autocracy, when the service of the nobility is necessary and needful for the common welfare, every honourable nobleman is obligated to respond to the first summons from the autocratic power and to spare neither his efforts nor his very life in serving the state.

The Charter made it clear that those nobles who neglected or rejected their service obligations would be treated as second-class members of their estate: 'A nobleman who has never been in service or who, having served, did not attain officer's rank . . . may be present at assemblies of the nobility; but he may not sit with the meritorious, may not vote in the assemblies of the nobility, and may not be elected to those posts filled by election of the assembly of the nobility.

How, then, may we summarize events in Russia between the deaths of her two great eighteenth-century rulers, Peter I and Catherine II? By the end of the century the nobility had emerged as a corporate, privileged class with legal guarantees of civil liberty. Superficially, therefore, they appeared to be shining exemplars of the Enlightened view of the law which sought to protect the subject against the arbitrariness of government. But the reality was quite contrary. The liberty of the nobles constituted the liberties of an estate or class and had significance precisely because other segments of the population, notably the serfs, did not share them. Legal inequality between groups of subjects was the hallmark of a polity in which the power of the impersonal state had not yet grown strong enough to impose the liberty as well as the tyranny of equal subjection on all. The Charter of 1785 marked the decisive stage in Russia's regression from the modern state idea. Thereafter she lagged behind *ancien régime* France. Revolution, which was shortly to overwhelm the latter, would be successfully resisted in Russia for another century and more. Without such upheavals, however, neither country's political system appeared capable of fostering the concept of the impersonal state.

## REFLECTIONS OF THE RUSSIAN NOBILITY: A. N. RADISHCHEV AND N. M. KARAMZIN

The effects of the Western Enlightenment and of eighteenth-century political developments in Russia on the outlook of Russian writers were dramatic. The spectacular history of the Russian *intelligentsiya* was just beginning. However, reactions were by no means uniform. It may be illuminating, therefore, to conclude this chapter with an examination of the equally mature yet differing perspectives and conclusions drawn by two distinguished commentators upon the political scene, A. N. Radishchev and N. M. Karamzin. Radishchev's *Journey from St. Petersburg to Moscow* and Karamzin's *Memoir on Ancient and Modern Russia* offer radical and conservative solutions to the dilemma of liberty versus authority that was so starkly posed in the Russian context.

The two men were of similar background. Both were brought up as noble scions on estates situated on the middle Volga, though Radishchev, born in 1749, was the elder by some seventeen years.

Both were educated in Moscow and both travelled in the West, Radishchev to Leipzig and Karamzin a good deal further afield, to Paris and London. Both therefore were familiar with major writers of the Enlightenment like Montesquieu and Rousseau. Each included Robertson among his favourite historians and the distinguished writer and publicist, Novikov, amongst his friends. Each wrote in his early forties a work of political philosophy which remains a significant contribution to an intractable problem. Yet neither was able, from mutually opposed standpoints to indicate a way forward which might reconcile the conflicting demands of men of property and men of burden, of government and society, of freedom and security.

The condition of Russia meant that neither Radishchev nor Karamzin enunciated, as Peter the Great long before had tried to do, the idea of the impersonal state as the ultimate arbiter of man's social existence. Radishchev set off in that direction by invoking the original social contract whereby free and equal men living in a state of nature voluntarily agreed to limit their freedom. The political implication of such a contract for Radishchev was the establishment of a civil order which would match the pristine equality of the natural man: 'But though all have accepted restrictions upon their freedom and submitted their acts to regulation, yet all, because in a state of nature they would have been equal from birth, must still be equal in the limitations set to their natural freedom.'[37] Clearly no such state of affairs obtained in Russia, where a sizeable proportion of the population had no civil rights at all. Radishchev put all his emphasis upon the right to liberty, supporting each individual's obligation to seek his own preservation, defence and welfare, a natural right which he regained if the equality of citizenship was denied to him. Despite the fact that his family had been perilously exposed during the *Pugachevshchina* he relegated the dangers of insecurity to a poor second after the pursuit of liberty, going so far as to imply that the property rights of the noble serf-owners could only be set aside by force. That was certainly the Empress Catherine's interpretation of his comments.[38]

The real enemy of liberty for Radishchev was the government: not the impersonal machine, but the tsar, shah, khan, king, bey, nabob, sultan or emperor. We know from another of his works that he equated the Russian word for autocracy, which in the eighteenth century also had the meaning of monarchy and sovereignty, with despotism.[39] For him law should have been the sovereign representative of all the people and the ruler merely its instrument. But how could the implementation of such a law be guaranteed, in the context of autocratic kingship which Radishchev assumed? Apparently only by the ruler's conversion to virtue, which Radishchev depicted in a dream sequence: 'I saw afresh the responsibility of my high office, recognized the vastness of my duty, and understood whence proceeded my right and power. I trembled inwardly and was terrified by the responsibility of my stewardship.'[40]

For Radishchev the pursuit of virtue was humanity's supreme aspiration and any society whose laws or customs thwarted it was to be defied. He scorned as weakness that 'prudence' to which men were inclined to resort when faced with the hostility of the majority. However, his utopian vision ignored the stresses imposed upon the political order by such behaviour. His invocation of suicide, which he was to choose himself, as the ultimate means of preserving individual honour against oppression suggested an idealistic spirit unwilling to compromise with political realities. Besides, as that supreme political pragmatist, Catherine the Great, observed, it was far from clear what Radishchev meant by virtue.[41]

Karamzin approached the problem from the opposite point of view, though he shared some of Radishchev's basic assumptions. He acknowledged an original covenant between the people and the ruler and the moral strength of regimes as well as their physical power. He believed that states, like human beings, grew, flourished and ultimately decayed. Radishchev had expressed the same idea thus: 'from tyranny, freedom is born; from freedom, slavery'.[42] But Karamzin viewed all these matters in the context of the nation's security, not of the liberty of its members. The people's contract with their sovereign, for example, required the latter to 'Guard our safety abroad and at home, punish criminals, sacrifice a part to save the whole.'[43] Similarly, he linked Russia's moral force with the proper disposition of her security needs, suggesting that Alexander I was more dishonoured by his gratuitous conquest of Finland for which he was reproached by all the other nations than by his defeat of Napoleon. Most significant of all, however, was Karamzin's interpretation of the pathology of states. He believed that it was only by maintaining her traditional autocracy that Russia could hope to prolong her national life. Yet that autocracy should be buttressed by the support of gentry and clergy, and by the Senate and Holy Synod as repositaries of the law. The noble estate in particular had a crucial role to play. Karamzin quoted Montesquieu's famous couplet: 'point de Monarque – point de noblesse; point de noblesse – point de Monarque', and he elaborated a view of the contractual relationship between tsar and noble of which the Frenchman would have thoroughly approved: 'The rights of the well-born are not something apart from monarchical authority – they are its principal and indispensable instrumentality by means of which the body politic is kept in motion.'[44]

This regime of estates, incorporating liberties for some, offered no hope of liberty for the majority. Characteristically Karamzin linked the issue of serfdom to that of the country's security: 'The primary obligation of the monarch is to safeguard the internal and external unity of the state; benefiting estates and individuals comes second. Alexander wishes to improve the lot of the peasants by granting them freedom; but what if this freedom should harm the state?' More bluntly still, and in language reminiscent of John Locke, he asserted that 'from the point of view of political stability it is safer to enslave men than to give them freedom prematurely'.[45] There was a Lockean ring, too, to his defence of noble land which he described as the lawful and inalienable property of the nobility. Karamzin was committed, in other words, to the status quo as offering the best hope of longevity to the Russian body politic.

Not surprisingly, neither Karamzin nor Radishchev was able to escape from the influences and traditions of his native environment. The latter's brave manifesto was aimed not against that contemporary political order but, somewhat unexpectedly, against that aspect of the Russian tradition which was represented by the old Muscovite tsardom, the pre-Petrine autocracy, which, to Radishchev's cultivated mind, was mere despotism. The vehemence of his support for individual liberty was a reaction against the insensitivity of that tradition to the human condition. Karamzin, on the other hand, reflected in his work the contractual relationship between ruler and nobility, culminating in the Charter of 1785, which equally inhibited the spread of political liberty because of the inequalities inherent in such a system of separate estates. Karamzin himself denied that Russians had ever possessed civil rights. 'We have only political rights,' he argued, 'that is the specific rights of the various estates of the realm; we have gentry, merchants, townsfolk, peasants, and so forth – they all enjoy their specific rights, but they have no right in common, save for that of calling themselves Russians.'[46]

Neither man contemplated the idea of the impersonal state which, with its requirement of equality between subjects, could provide a degree of political liberty for the individual within the framework of a truly awesome autocracy. Radishchev, in particular, like his French contemporary, Condorcet, aspired to an unflawed freedom which was no more attainable than that sought by Russia's Cossack bands in the sixteenth and seventeenth centuries.

## REFERENCES AND NOTES

1.  Brenda Meehan-Waters, *Autocracy and Aristocracy: the Russian service elite of 1730* (New Brunswick 1982), pp. 138–45.
2.  G. Vernadsky *et al* (eds), *A Source Book for Russian History from Early Times to 1917*, 3 vols (London 1972), II, p. 378.
3.  Meehan-Waters, *op. cit.*, p. 145.

4.   *Ibid.*, p. 236, note 34.
5.   Marc Raeff, *Plans for Political Reform in Imperial Russia, 1730–1905* (Englewood Cliffs, New Jersey 1966), p. 50.
6.   S. M. Troitsky, *Russky Absolyutizm i Dvoryanstvo b XVII b.* (Moscow 1974), pp. 141–2.
7.   Raeff, *Russian Intelligentsia*, p. 148.
8.   Pipes, *Russia under the Old Regime* (London 1977 edn), p. 127. *Karamzin's Memoir on Ancient and Modern Russia*, ed. Richard Pipes (Cambridge, Mass. 1959), p. 45.
9.   Raeff, *Russian Intelligentsia*, p. 155. Marc Raeff, 'The Enlightenment in Russia and Russian thought in the Enlightenment', *The Eighteenth Century in Russia*, ed. J. G. Garrard (Oxford 1973), pp. 35 ff. W. J. Gleason, *Moral Idealists, Bureaucracy and Catherine the Great* (New Brunswick New Jersey 1981), pp. 58–9.
10.  For the hidden influence of Adam Smith on Catherine II see Paul Dukes, *Catherine the Great's Instruction (Nakaz) to the Legislative Commission, 1767*: Vol. II of *Russia under Catherine the Great* (Newtonville, Mass. 1977), pp. 19–20.
11.  This last theme is interestingly explored by Hans Rogger, *National Consciousness in Eighteenth Century Russia* (Cambridge Mass. 1960).
12.  Cf. the comments by Dukes, *Catherine the Great's Instruction*, pp. 15–16.
13.  M. M. Shcherbatov, *On the Corruption of Morals in Russia*, ed. and transl. A. Lentin (Cambridge 1969), p. 113.
14.  See the particularly relevant observations by Marc Raeff, 'The well-ordered police state and the development of modernity in seventeenth and eighteenth century Europe: an attempt at a comparative approach', *American Historical Review*, 80 (1975), 1230–3.
15.  The Table is reproduced by James Hassell, 'Implementation of the Russian Table of Ranks during the eighteenth century', *Slavic Review*, 29 (1970), 284.
16.  *Ibid.*, p. 289. Paul Dukes, *Catherine the Great and the Russian Nobility* (Cambridge 1967), pp. 44–5.
17.  Vernadsky, *op. cit.*, II, p. 392.
18.  Robert E. Jones, *The Emancipation of the Russian Nobility, 1762–1785* (Princeton 1973), pp. 33 ff.
19.  *Ibid.*, p. 90.
20.  *Ibid.*, p. 64. Dukes, *Catherine the Great and the Russian Nobility*, p. 13.
21.  Dukes, *Catherine the Great and the Russian Nobility*, p. 45, quotes the telling observation of the Russian historian, S. A. Korf, writing in 1906: 'So it normally happens in life, and particularly when dealing with the understanding of freedom. It is repellent to man to do what he is compelled to do.'
22.  Isobel de Madariaga, *Russia in the Age of Catherine the Great* (London 1981), p. 151.
23.  Dukes, *Catherine the Great's Instruction*, p. 54.
24.  *Ibid.*, p. 46.
25.  *Ibid.*, p. 58.
26.  *Ibid.*, pp. 43–4. cf. Baron de Montesquieu *De l'esprit des lois, Oeuvres complètes*, edn du Seuil (Paris 1964), Book 8, ch. 19.
27.  Dukes, *Catherine the Great's Instruction*, p. 44.

28.  Rogger, *op. cit.*, p. 34.
29.  Dukes, *Catherine the Great's Instruction*, p. 11.
30.  *Ibid.*, p. 77.
31.  The events of the *Pugachevshchina* may be followed in John Alexander, *Autocratic Politics in a National Crisis: the Imperial Russian government and Pugachev's revolt, 1773–1775* (Bloomington, Indiana 1969), *passim*.
32.  Vernadsky, *op. cit.*, II, pp. 454–5.
33.  Madariaga, *op. cit.*, p. 286.
34.  Jones, *op. cit.*, pp. 267–8.
35.  Abbreviated versions of the Statute for the Administration of the Provinces and the Charter of the Nobility may be found in Vernadsky, *op. cit.*, II, pp. 410–11, 413–15.
36.  Madariaga, *op. cit.*, p. 299.
37.  A. N. Radishchev, *A Journey from St. Petersburg to Moscow*, ed. R. P. Thaler (Cambridge, Mass. 1958), p. 145.
38.  *Ibid.*, pp. 102, 191, 248.
39.  *Ibid.*, p. 66. Madariaga, *op. cit.*, p. xi. The other work in question is Radishchev's translation of Mably's *Observations sur l'histoire de la Grèce*: see the Introduction to *A Journey from St. Petersburg to Moscow*, p. 6.
40.  *Ibid.*, p. 76.
41.  *Ibid.*, p. 244.
42.  *Ibid.*, p. 200.
43.  Pipes, *Karamzin's Memoir on Ancient and Modern Russia*, p. 122.
44.  *Ibid.*, pp. 146, 200.
45.  *Ibid.*, p. 166. Note, too, the observation by Immanuel Kant, *What is Enlightenment? Kant on history*, ed. L. W. Beck (New York 1963), p. 10, that the people only gradually 'become capable of managing freedom'.
46.  Pipes, *Karamzin's Memoir on Ancient and Modern Russia*, p. 185.

# Chapter seven

# RUSSIA'S WESTERN AND NORTHERN NEIGHBOURS

## THE POLISH 'COMMONWEALTH'

A comparison with several of Russia's western and northern neighbours serves to counterpoint the dominant Muscovite motif. Poland, or from 1569 the Commonwealth of Poland-Lithuania, seems at first sight to have had a good deal in common with her eastern rival. By the time that the first Romanov was governing Muscovy, the territorial dimensions and the populations of the two countries were very similar. Both rulers faced the problem of maintaining their authority over vast tracts of land, much of it sparsely populated. In both countries too serfdom had become the characteristic feature of socio-economic relationships for the overwhelming mass of the population. The priority given to the possession of land inhibited the kind of urban growth which was to be so prominent a feature of Western European development between the sixteenth and eighteenth centuries. Finally, Poland possessed a deep religious commitment and tradition to rival that of the Third Rome. After 1453, when Constantinople fell to Islam, Poland's already well-established role as the final bulwark of Christendom in the east was reinforced. The ideology of Western, Roman Catholicism would henceforth be levelled against the power of Islam, and later against that of Russian Orthodoxy.

However, in terms of the present argument the contrast between Muscovy and her oldest enemy looms far larger than these comparisons. A complex set of circumstances fashioned a political development in the Polish Commonwealth, the *Rzeczpospolita*, which was diametrically opposed to that of her eastern neighbour.

Part of the explanation lies with the lack of ideological commitment to the Polish crown. Kings of Poland had none of the religious charisma of the saintly grand dukes and tsars of Muscovy, despite their country's centuries-old reputation as the champion of Christendom. Paradoxically this fact may have been due in part to the very success of the Polish kings in greatly increasing the bounds of their authority. From the end of the fourteenth century plans were devised for the incorporation of the Grand Duchy of Lithuania into the Polish kingdom. Eventually the union was formally sealed by the Treaty of Lublin (1569) which stipulated that henceforth the two territories should be ruled by a single, elected ruler. The effect was to add to Poland's eastern flank an enormous wedge of land stretching to the frontier of Muscovy. The sheer size of the new 'Commonwealth', its capacity to defend itself with relative ease against weaker neighbours, deprived it of that sense of crusading zeal which sometimes surfaces in more embattled regimes. Both Sweden and Muscovy seemed for a long time to be the puniest of neighbours when measured against a state which joined the Black Sea to the Baltic.

Besides, the union with Lithuania brought a number of non-Catholic influences into the Polish world. Lithuania had remained pagan far longer than any other European state – its Grand Duke was only converted to Catholicism late in the fourteenth century – and numbers of Orthodox christians became members of the Commonwealth as a result of the Treaty of Lublin. After the German Reformation Protestantism entered Poland from the West, while Polish Jewry had been established before Polish Christianity. There was an evident need for toleration which made it difficult for the kings of Poland-Lithuania to assert the kind of psychological domination that went with the title of *Gosudar'*. There was one other reason why toleration made more sense in Poland than militant Christian action. For much of the later Middle Ages the Poles had fought bitter campaigns against fellow Catholics, the crusading Knights of Livonia.[1]

Nor were the kings of Poland-Lithuania able to control the land-owners as the Russian rulers with their grants of *pomest'e* estates were able to do. This was because the Polish nobility had sources of wealth which made them independent of royal service. At about the time that Ivan the Great of Moscow (1462–1505) was quickening the long process of gathering in the Russian lands to the Riurik dynasty, the Polish grain trade up the Vistula to Danzig and westwards to Amsterdam and beyond was beginning to enrich great magnates amongst the Polish nobility. The boom lasted well into the seventeenth century. It was sustained by rising prices in the West, by the expansion of great noble estates in the Ukraine and by the widespread enserfment of free peasant holdings. The precise connection between the nobility's economic efflorescence and the advance of serfdom in the Commonwealth remains a matter of considerable historical debate. However, few would disagree with the observation of the most recent English-speaking historian of Poland, Norman Davies, that 'it would be foolish to deny that the spectacular growth of the export trade in grain was accompanied by an equally marked rise in the conditions of serfdom, and that in one way or another these twin socio-economic developments of the sixteenth and early seventeenth centuries were closely connected'.[2] Yet the Polish historian, Topolski, is also surely right to point out that only the largest-scale producers could afford to ship grain over such vast distances and still make a profit.[3] Most of the *szlachta* produced grain for the internal market, though in this sphere too the growth of serfdom appears to have been a necessary corollary. In Poland this latter development arose as a result of noble pressure and not, as in Muscovy, of government policy. Behind that fact lay the crucial distinction between the service relationship of the *pomeshchiki* to the tsar and the increasingly domineering attitude of the *szlachta* to the Polish king.[4] The difference may be accounted for by the relative security of Poland-Lithuania, which had the effect of weakening the crown's hold on its nobility, and the persistence, nevertheless, of expensive wars. In 1569 the Crown owned a mere 15 per cent of the land, and so the king was forced, when he needed additional revenue, to turn to the noble class for assistance. They were quick to extract economic and political advantages in return for their support.[5]

By the time of the Treaty of Lublin the Polish nobility had acquired a number of political privileges. It formed a separate estate, securely buttressed by a long sequence of legislative acts. No new tax could be levied, for example, or army raised without the consent of the local noble dietines; no non-noble could own land. In 1493, the central bicameral Diet or *Sejm* was established, and in 1505 the statute of *Nihil Novi* ruled that no new laws could be introduced without the agreement of both chambers. Since the nobility monopolized the membership of both houses, it had effectively procured control over the legislative process. It was a relatively simple matter thereafter for the nobility to acquire a succession of further liberties at the expense of an increasingly unfree peasant population, bound to their lords' will without even the recourse of appeal to the royal courts.

A further contributing factor to the *szlachta*'s fierce sense of independence was a deeply felt psychological conviction that all the members of their estate shared a precious equality which was part of the liberty of being a nobleman of the Commonwealth. The economic reality, of course, was quite different. That was to be expected, but in a world shaped by considerations of legal exclusivity it did not greatly matter. Indeed, the very inequality underscored the nobles' sense of corporate solidarity – the word applies as justly to them as to the banned trade-unionists of the present day. Their juridical homogeneity was unmatched in early modern Europe.[6] It reflected a self-confidence and an independence which would increasingly threaten royal authority. After Lublin all the privileges of the Polish nobility were acquired by their Lithuanian counterparts.

The final, and the decisive factor favouring the predominance of the nobility in the Commonwealth, was the extinction of the Jagiellonian line with the death of Sigismund II in 1572. From that date until Poland's disappearance from the map of Europe following the Third Partition of 1795, her monarchy was elective and her monarch's powers were heavily circumscribed. The Jagiellonian period lasted from the late fourteenth century, when Poland and Lithuania were first united under the Lithuanian Grand-Duke, Jagiello, to 1572 when the death of Sigismund II (Zygmunt in Polish) allowed the elective procedure forecast in the Treaty of Lublin to take effect. In theory the Polish Crown had remained elective throughout the period, but since the Jagiellons were hereditary grand dukes of Lithuania, their election to the Polish throne had become a formality. In 1572, however, when the last member of the dynasty died, the election acquired new significance.

The highly self-conscious noble order seized the political opportunity presented to it in 1572 to dictate its own terms to the successors of the Jagiellonian line. Like Catherine the Great's Charter of the Nobility, the Polish contract spelled out with such clarity the terms of the agreement that there would henceforth be little room for manoeuvre, even when the status quo threatened the country's survival. Unlike the Russian model, the Polish variant was heavily biased against the monarchy. It was embodied principally in the Henrician Articles of 1573 which were presented by the noble Diet to the French prince Henry of Valois, who had to suscribe to them as a condition of his election to the vacant throne. All his elected successors had to adhere in their turn to the same articles. These constitutional constraints imposed upon successive rulers the obligation to summon the Diet every two years; not to declare war, raise taxes or summon the nobility for military service without the Diet's approval; not to take measures to hinder the nobility's freedom to elect in the future the kings of their choice; and to recognize the nobility's right of resistance if the king contravened his oath to maintain the Henrician Articles. The secondary contract between the Crown and the nobility was agreed at the second election in 1576, when the Transylvanian prince, Stefan Bathory, became king of Poland. This was the *Pacta Conventa* which in Bathory's case concerned matters of foreign policy and the national debt. Subsequently, however, the terms of the *Pacta Conventa*, unlike those of the Henrician Articles, changed from reign to reign to take into account particular circumstances about which the nobility required assurances.

The result was that from 1572 until Poland's final dissolution in 1795, the nobility lived in what may be described as a quasi-natural state in which the pursuit of personal and civic liberty was given an absolute priority. If one applies the idea of the social contract in both its social and political form to the Polish nobility, one cannot but conclude that they were as anxious to re-establish conditions approaching those of the state of nature, for themselves at least, as they were to escape from them. They embraced their concept of liberty so single-mindedly that it became anarchy. The right of confederation, 'a legalized form of civil war'[7], allowed nobles to band together to achieve their aims, as happened in 1656 and 1672 and on six further occasions during the eighteenth century. The most notorious of all the Polish freedoms was the *Liberum Veto*, the right of any member of the Diet to invalidate legislation of which he disapproved by using his vote to bring the assembly to a close. Such a practice frustrated the formulation of any coherent policies which might have rescued the Commonwealth from disaster at some cost to noble liberties. It also allowed those neighbouring powers, especially Russia which would ultimately consummate Poland's destruction, to keep her in a state of weakness through agents whose invocation of the veto could be cynically supported as maintaining Poland's 'golden freedom'.[8]

Even in their attitude to the law the Commonwealth nobility showed a willingness to flout the conventions of civil society. Nobles frequently ignored the courts, waged private wars and had a tendency to take the law into their own hands. Civil disorder was rife. One is reminded again of Hobbes' definition of war in the state of nature which consisted 'not in actual fighting; but in the known disposition thereto during all the time there is no assurance to the contrary'.[9] This world of near-anarchy was the product of that unrestrained liberty against which John Locke warned in his *Second Treatise of Government*.

Finally, it should be recalled that this regime of transcendant liberty was based upon the enserfment of the larger part of the population. Again the analogy with the state of nature becomes compelling. In such a state one would expect the strong to impose their authority upon the weak in order to maintain their own freedom of action. In the last two centuries of its existence, the *Rzeczpospolita* became a land of noble 'cossacks' and peasant serfs. This combination of extremes undermined the country's viability as surely as the original cossack-serf dichotomy has threatened the security of old Muscovy. By the eighteenth century Poland's internal weaknesses, compounded by economic decline, had fully exposed her vulnerability to neighbours now far more powerful than herself. The demand for Polish grain in the West had fallen, and from 1648 war regularly devastated the Commonwealth's land.[10] But it was pre-eminently the Crown's inability to regain the political initiative which prevented any sort of economic or political revival. Poland-Lithuania was incapable of raising an army large and powerful enough to deter aggression; nor had she ever developed a diplomatic corps capable of keeping her government informed of international opinion.[11] The nobility turned increasingly xenophobic, embracing the so-called Sarmatian cult which identified them with the descendants of the ancient Sarmatae tribe.[12] This sense of exclusivism fed their dreams of perfect liberty at the moment of their country's supreme crisis. The Polish Commonwealth was about to succumb to regimes on her borders which did not permit the privileges of groups of citizens to threaten the security of their realms. Like the Dutch burgher class, but with more dramatic results, the nobility of Poland-Lithuania were embarked on the road to political suicide. In 1772 Russia, approaching its own 'golden age of the nobility', and having already annexed the Polish words for 'Diet' and 'Nobility' to its own vocabulary, joined the Austrians and Prussians in the first partition of Poland. Catherine II was thus able to regain parts of White Russia which had belonged to the Kievan state in the days before the Mongol invasions. The second and third partitions, completing the Commonwealth's destruction, followed in 1793 and 1795.

Before the partitions took their effect, however, the Polish Commonwealth had already been mortally wounded by the unshakeable adherence of its own elite to a concept of absolute freedom which flouted political reality. Such an inflexible outlook had already doomed Russian cossackdom and a similarly uncompromising view of liberty, though approached from a very different standpoint, would also drive Alexander Radishchev, himself a 'cossack' in that regard, along the road to self-destruction.

## THE EXPERIENCE OF SWEDEN

During the seventeenth century Sweden took Poland's place as the chief enemy of the Russian state. That rivalry reached its climax in the Great Northern War (1700–21), in the course of which Peter the Great destroyed Sweden's Baltic Empire. Despite this mutual enmity, the tsar found much to admire in his rival's administrative system and much of his collegiate reform programme was based upon the Swedish model.[13] Yet there were enormous differences in the socio-political structures and traditions of the two countries. The Vasa dynasty, with its Protestant-based ideology, could invoke a tradition of strong kingship, though its power reflected but palely that of the *tishaishii* tsar. For Sweden also evolved a form of constitutional opposition to absolutism led by the great magnates, which, with the principle of elective monarchy, might at first sight suggest that Sweden occupied a halfway position between Russia and Poland. That, however, would be a misleading representation for a number of reasons.

There was no history of serfdom in Sweden. There was a free peasantry which was represented in the Swedish parliament or

*Riksdag*. From the early sixteenth century this body had become a permanent part of the Swedish constitution. It contained the representatives of four estates, the nobility, the clergy and the burghers as well as the peasants. The appearance of the *Riksdag* underlined the long tradition in Sweden of the legal basis of the political order. It is in that context that the doyen of British historians of Sweden, Michael Roberts, has pointed out how much there is in common between Swedish history and that of Britain.[14]

The founder of independent Sweden, Gustav Vasa, was elected king by the *Riksdag* in 1523. Buttressed by the establishment of a Lutheran state church and by the additional revenues which were diverted to secular purposes, Gustav was able, in 1544, to strengthen his family's hold upon the Crown. In that year the *Riksdag* approved the Succession Pact which declared the crown to be hereditary in the Vasa line.

But security within Sweden's frontiers was not yet matched by security in the Baltic region as a whole. Gustav Vasa's successors began to stretch their inheritance around the Baltic shores as the best means of guaranteeing external stability. The rise and fall of the Swedish Empire (1560–1721) made the kings of Sweden military leaders first and foremost. As they fought against the other Baltic powers, Denmark, Muscovy, Poland and Brandenburg in an ultimately unsuccessful bid to secure strategic and economic hegemony, they projected an image of kingship favourable to the development of absolutism.[15] Yet even in the light of Sweden's chronic insecurity, that experience did not persuade them to resort unequivocally to absolutism, at least until the Empire was in terminal decline under Charles XII (1697–1718). Examples of such conduct under the Vasas were rare. Gustav Vasa's son, Eric XIV (1560–68) revealed an absolutism 'more obvious, more explicit and more capricious than his father's',[16] and he was eventually deposed. In 1600 Charles IX triumphed bloodily over the opposition of aristocratic constitutionalists at the so-called Massacre of Linköping. Yet despite these episodes the counter-claims of constitutional monarchy invariably re-asserted themselves.

The starting point for this powerful tradition was Magnus Erikson's Land Law of about 1350. This was Sweden's first general lawcode. It also defined the constitution, stipulating that the Crown should be elective and laying down a legal basis for its relationship with the subjects. Its principles were incorporated in the Coronation oath which required the king to accept the law of the land and not to establish new laws without the people's consent. His right to impose taxation was also set in a consultative framework.[17] In 1594 Sigismund III went further by granting an Accession Charter, linked to the recognition of his kingship, and between the beginning of Gustav Adolph's reign in 1611 and that of Charles XII in 1697, the principle of the ruler's obligation to make these additional promises at the time of their accession was consistently adhered to. It was a portent of Charles XII's authoritarian intent that in 1697 he should refuse to subscribe to an Accession Charter.[18]

Even Charles XI (1660–97) scrupulously maintained his respect for the law despite the growth of absolutism during his reign. Transactions in Sweden were still most frequently conducted in kind so that money was scarce. The country's security depended upon its armed forces and on the availability of resources additional to those drawn from the Crown lands. This was especially so as the Empire faced decline. Consequently the *Riksdag* of 1680 was persuaded to grant Charles XI a *reduktion*, the right to reclaim royal land which had been given away to the nobility. This measure increased the king's financial independence from the *Riksdag*. The latter also assured him that as king he should consider himself responsible to God alone. Nevertheless, Charles did not avail himself of this freedom to evade the earthly law of his kingdom, so potent was the tradition of Magnus Erikson's Land Law.[19]

These competing lines of development, offering unfettered royal authority on the one hand and constitutional monarchy clearly set out in legal terms on the other, ultimately produced neither a Russian nor a Polish-type polity. The abiding strength of each tradition prevented the complete triumph of either. Noble liberties were not to be enforced at the expense of a servile peasantry. The lower estates of the *Riksdag* were prepared on occasion to ally with the Crown against the noble estate. Indeed, the king was generally popular. His personal authority was welcomed as a guarantee against the excesses of over-mighty subjects.[20] Conversely, the development of a national army billeted on the land in peacetime inhibited any royal recourse to force.

The army's close links with the population at large is of particular significance when seeking the origins of impersonal statehood. Not only was it 'one of the most powerful negative factors in securing the survival of popular liberties, and in shoring up the concept of the rule of law'[21], it was also a powerful positive element in giving unity and identity to a state permanently at risk from predatory neighbours. Earlier than in any other European country the Swedish infantry had evolved as a national conscript force based upon provincial levies. From the reign of Gustav Adolph the number of men to be recruited annually was decided by the *Riksdag*. It was also in that reign that the practice was established of allocating a plot of land for each conscript to which he could return in peacetime. This system was fully worked out in the *indelningsverket*, or allotment system of Charles XI, whereby the provinces guaranteed to raise the necessary number of men and to provide them with land and accommodation.[22] The distinctive method in which the Swedish army was organized, so different from the feudal levy or the mercenary force, suggests that the precocious idea of service to an abstract state was not so far away.

Though it would be an over-simplification to portray the two traditions of government as mutually hostile, yet with the decline and dissolution of the Swedish Empire the two strands did emerge as openly antagonistic alternatives. The growing absolutism of Charles XI's reign was followed by the full-blooded authoritarianism of Charles XII. After the latter's premature death in battle in 1718 the pendulum swung in favour of constitutionalism. The so-called Age of Liberty lasted until 1772 when the *coup d'état* of Gustav III re-asserted monarchical authority.

The reaction of 1718 was made more effective by the absence of a direct heir to Charles XII. The *Riksdag* seized the opportunity to re-state an old principle by declaring Charles's sister, Ulrica Eleonora the elected queen (1718–20). In 1720 her husband was similarly elected as Frederick I (1720–51). In the period that followed parliamentary ascendancy ensured that 'The King had become nothing more than the chief member of the Council, and his in-fluence was limited to the exercise of two votes on important issues.'[23]

Initially, the new parliamentary regime was still based on noble privilege and on the natural inequalities between subjects. But new pressures were beginning to be felt as the ideas of the Enlightenment reached Sweden. Writers like Anders Nordencrantz (1697–1772) called for the abolition of privilege and the establishment of a free press to guarantee universal liberty.[24] Such views coincided with a shift from effective aristocratic hegemony to the rule of the Estates. In the mid-1760s the more radical 'Caps' party gained power from the rival 'Hats'. The Caps had developed a party organization and policy which linked the *Riksdag* more directly to the electorate, especially those of the burgher estate. Their programme called for greater parliamentary accountability, notably *via* a free press, the enforce-ment in the *Riksdag* of binding election mandates, and the elimination from government of unnecessary secrecy. They were also economic liberals, opposed to large-scale exporters, whose mercantilist principles dominated the Hats' political philosophy. Thus they broke Stockholm's trade monopoly between the Gulf of Bothnia and foreign ports and gave Swedish farmers the freedom to transport their produce to any part of the kingdom.[25]

However, the Cap party was not committed to a root and branch reform which would introduce a regime of political equality. Among its chief ideologues only Henrik Lemstrom called for the elimination of all privileges.[26] Nevertheless, it did represent itself as a radical party committed to the under-privileged, and in the wake of its reformist programme came demands on behalf of those who were too lowly even to be represented by the peasant estate. In 1770

Alexander Kepplerus protested on behalf of the landless labourers that all men should have equal liberty.[27] Such claims naturally alarmed all the privileged groups in Swedish society and helped to create an atmosphere conducive to Gustav III's resumption of absolute royal authority. Yet by that stage, 1772, there could be no longer any question of a simple resumption of royal power as it had been exercised under Charles XI or Charles XII. Gustav III embarked upon a reign of enlightened absolutism, 'which may be described as being by Mercier de la Rivière out of *The Patriot King*'.[28] Events gradually pushed him towards a regime of political and social equality. The lower estates acquired equal rights with the nobility to most public offices, including places in the newly established High Court which succeeded the once all-powerful noble Council as the chief court of appeal. Most types of land became available for purchase by commoners, and peasants were given the absolute right to dispose as they pleased of their farms and land. Restrictions on their rights to hunt and fish and to employ their own servants were abolished. His 'path towards equal privileges for all', as one Swedish historian has characterized the reign, edged Sweden towards that legal equality in the citizens' relationship to the government which was a concomitant of abstract statehood.[29] That process was temporarily halted in 1792 by a noble assassin's bullet.

Early modern Sweden was an anomaly. Though its fiscal and commercial life, like that of Russia, was unsophisticated, its political organization, like that of Britain, was complex and precocious. During the Age of Liberty the *Riksdag* developed a genuine party system and the ability to operate subtle constitutional conventions.[30] Indeed by the end of the eighteenth century Sweden had moved significantly in the direction of the impersonal state idea. The role of the army has already been mentioned in this regard. There is a second factor, however, which Sweden shared most notably with Britain. The complexity of her political traditions and institutions tended to obfuscate the location of sovereign power. Where in Sweden did sovereignty reside? Was it with the king or with the *Riksdag*? That was still an unanswered question when, in 1789 of all dates, Gustav III signed the Act of Union and Security giving him absolute power in matters of peace and war but leaving the *Riksdag* with the power of the purse. If both governing traditions were to be accommodated, sovereign authority would in fact have to reside in their joint action. The sanction for such action would have to transcend the interests of each element in the constitution. The state as an abstract idea was at hand. In 1809, at the height of the Napoleonic Wars, Sweden produced a written constitution which survives as the basis of the modern state. It retained the medieval representative principle of four estates in the *Riksdag* but that anachronism only disguised the new system's essential modernity. The balance between king and *Riksdag* owed more to Swedish history than to the theory of Montesquieu. It left the king in executive charge and the *Riksdag*, which was to be summoned at least every five years, free to reject royal legislation and budgetary proposals. There was also to be freedom of the press, of speech and religion.[31]

This constitution was an attempt to restore order and security at home and abroad. Gustav IV had been deposed by a civil and military *coup* in March 1809, and the country was at war with France, Russia and Denmark-Norway. In less than a month the constitution was drafted and approved by a committee of the *Riksdag*. The internal crisis ended with the election of the new king, Charles XIII, and his acceptance of the constitution. The king retained a powerful role but he had been elected and there was an unmistakeable threat in the estates' preamble to the constitution. There it was noted that they, as 'the Swedish people's delegates, entered into the right to improve the fatherland's situation in the future through the establishment of a changed state constitution'.[32] In post-Revolutionary Europe the concept of the abstract state was hailed in tones tinged with patriotic fervour but there was no disguising the idea itself. In 1809 internal insecurity was banished by a regime in which the subjects' political freedom was given a high priority, in the spirit of Sweden's own multi-form constitutional tradition. Only Britain could rival that emphasis.

## THE GERMAN ENLIGHTENMENT

Finally, a set of variations was worked out in eighteenth-century Germany where the ideas of the *Aufklärung* bring us part of the way back across the continent towards France. Only part of the way, however: for the German Enlightenment must not be identified with its West European counterpart. There were significant differences in both timing and emphasis which gave the *Aufklärung* its uniqueness.

Similarly, Germany itself represented a different kind of model from that of any other political structure in Europe. Unlike Russia, Poland or Sweden, it had no single identity though it formed a geographical entity and shared a common historical tradition. A balance of power was maintained in the region by a series of alliances, between neighbours within the *Reich*, secular and spiritual powers and the Imperial cities, and with outside powers. The greatest dynasty in Germany, the Habsburgs, ruled over territories outside the limits of the historic German lands, in Hungary, Italy and Transylvania, and in parts of Poland in the period after the partitions. Problems of security, therefore, could not be resolved merely by reference to a central controlling government authority.

By the eighteenth century the German lands were dominated by absolute princes who governed in co-operation with their noble subjects. The former guaranteed the latter's social and economic privileges, including in most regions the ownership of serfs. Serfdom was the dominant socio-economic form in the dynastic lands of the Habsburgs and Hohenzollerns, as well as in the lesser principalities like Baden and Württemberg, Hanover, Bavaria and Saxony. The closeness of the relationship between prince and noble varied from state to state. In Brandenburg-Prussia the relatively poor Junkers, who farmed estates that were far less profitable and extensive than those in Poland, suffered greatly from the ravages of the Thirty Years' War and the Northern War which followed in 1655. Their sense of insecurity was shared by the Great Elector of Brandenburg, himself no more than 'a super-Junker', in Rosenberg's phrase, before the peace of Westphalia in 1648.[33] Thereafter, beginning with the Recess of 1653, which was the formal outcome of a meeting between the deputies of the estates of Brandenburg and the Elector, Frederick William forged a contract with his nobility that enabled him and his successors to recruit the Junkers as officers into the Brandenburg-Prussian army and as bureaucrats into the new offices of state. He allowed the further institutionalization of serfdom and granted the noble class tax-freedom and a monopoly of landownership. But he also deprived the estates of Brandenburg and Prussia of their traditional liberty to vote public taxes.[34] Thus the basic principle of inequality peculiar to the *ständestaat*, a regime characterized by princely cooperation with the estates, in which the latter were dominated by the nobility, was stretched further in the interest of state security.

In most other parts of Germany a similar pattern could be discerned, of increasing central government authority at the expense of noble-dominated estates, though not precisely on the Prussian model. In the Habsburg lands, for example, the nobles were not so committed to the military ethos that distinguished their Junker equivalents.[35] Until late in the eighteenth century, however, the nobility's privileges, their social and territorial pre-eminence, remained free from threat despite the loss of institutional authority. What then was the impact of the German *Aufklärung* upon this dauntingly aristocratic and hierarchical world?

For most of the eighteenth century the thrust of the *Aufklärung* was reformist rather than radical. It accepted the principle of the *ständestaat*, modified as it had been by the rise of the princes. It did not seek, therefore, the political liberty of all subjects based upon their equal rights. It was more inclined to pursue less tangible, spiritual freedoms. In particular, the *aufklärers* were preoccupied with the issue of religious liberty. The application of reason – a fundamental trait of the Enlightenment everywhere – to contemporary questions reinforced the ideal of religious toleration, especially in Brandenburg-Prussia. Reason persuaded Frederick the Great that toleration would produce a more tranquil society than persecution ever could, and that there was no clash between the subject's inner freedom of the spirit and his bounden loyalty to the political sovereign.[36] By Frederick's reign the University of Halle, which was founded in 1694 by his grandfather, the Elector Frederick III, later King Frederick I, had become a European stronghold of rationalism. However, the tradition of toleration pre-dated the *Aufklärung*. Since 1613 the ruling Hohenzollern dynasty had been Calvinist in a largely Lutheran world. The Great Elector (1640–88) had practised a policy of Protestant toleration from the mid-seventeenth century. In this he was much influenced by the neostoical teaching of the Dutch humanist, Justus Lipsius (1547–1606), according to whom 'No king can command hearts as he commands tongues.'[37] Frederick the Great was more cynical. He expressed hostility to religious bigotry but his exercise of religious toleration was based upon personal indifference to religion. However, it was not until 1781 that Joseph II introduced this form of liberty into the Catholic Habsburg monarchy, and even at that late date in the eighteenth century there remained strong enclaves of opposition. The imperial city of Cologne held out until 1795 when it succumbed to the libertarian fervour of the French revolutionary armies.[38] There was no tradition of toleration in Catholic Germany of the kind that of necessity had grown up amongst the Protestant states.

There were other kinds of freedom espoused by writers of the German Enlightenment, but in order to comprehend them fully it is first necessary to discover what kind of people represented the *Aufklärung*. The German universities, headed by Halle and Göttingen, flourished in the eighteenth century and became not only centres of the Enlightenment but also training grounds for civil servants. Their graduates had an academic professional outlook that spanned the conventional gulf between noble and non-noble. Because most of them worked in government they were not disposed to attack the status quo with the same animosity as the French *philosophes*, who remained outsiders in *ancien régime* France.[39] Yet their training inculcated a reforming zeal which related directly to the business of political administration. They resolved their dilemma by maintaining their support for the concept of *ständestaat*, with its tradition of corporate liberties and by adding to that concept a generalized ideal of liberty which, though not fully realizable, ought nevertheless to inform the working of all well-ordered states. Thus they accepted whatever form of government existed, but sought to improve the reality of its relationships with the people, its spirit, by a variety of reforming measures: the abolition of serfdom, the alleviation of poverty, the introduction of a measure of free trade, the re-organization of the legal system.[40] In Krieger's apt phrase, this was 'a commitment to the fundamentals of the existing political system and a subscription to a transcendant ideal of freedom with which to judge it'.[41]

It should be remembered in addition that from the beginning of the Lutheran Reformation in Germany a sense of identity had existed between the ruler, his religion and that of his subjects. The doctrine of *cuius regio eius religio*, which was formally adopted at the Peace of Augsburg in 1555, defined the state in religious as well as in dynastic terms. That decision at once added an ethical dimension to the exercise of secular authority in Germany, just as the defence of the Third Rome did in Muscovy. At first the result was purely to reinforce the doctrinal status quo. In the longer term however, the possibility existed for the secular power to replace narrow confessional interests with a universal ethic. This line of argument implied a liberating role for the state itself; and of course a model of statehood far removed from dynastic principles. The state was described by the *aufklärers* in both mechanistic and organic terms. August Ludwig von Schlözer, one of Göttingen's most distinguished professors, combined the two metaphors thus: 'No institution lasts forever; no decree is eternal . . . In this manner, too, is the state a machine. Its wheels wear down; some become useless; its driving force falters . . . Soon new and more wheels are needed; new powers that before were not visible manifest themselves . . . The larger the state, the more it is a compound machine'.[42]

The writers of the German Enlightenment sought spiritual freedom within this complex mechanism. They also looked for a degree of economic liberty. Governments themselves began to support the entrepreneurial activities of their subjects, giving greater freedom of action to their merchants and manufacturers at the expense of municipal monopolies and local interests. The work of Adam Smith entered Germany with the enthusiastic backing of the University of Göttingen.[43] Yet policies of economic liberalism were invariably subordinated to the wider interests of state which had dictated their promulgation in the first place. We are therefore forced back to the conclusion already indicated above, that in Germany, and especially in Protestant Germany, the subjects' expectation of freedom depended increasingly upon the liberating function of the state.

In German universities that argument was developed during the eighteenth century. At Halle, Christian Thomasius outlined his vision of a *kulturstaat*, the state as a moral entity and the only setting in which the individual could fully realize his freedom.[44] That idea later reached its apotheosis in Berlin in the writings of Hegel. However, political realities in Germany did not match the smooth evolution of idealist theory. In Prussia the death of Frederick the Great briefly permitted the bureaucracy to come into its own as 'The servants of the state' and 'professional officials of the state'[45], but almost immediately the French Revolution and then the rise of Napoleon demonstrated the fundamental weakness of the Hohenzollern state. With its narrow military base, which depended upon a system of privilege for the Junkers at the expense of the peasant population, it compared unfavourably as a *kulturstaat* with France's revolutionary regime. Even in military terms it was no match for the Napoleonic forces which destroyed the old Prussian state at Jena in 1806. At the time Hegel was a professor at the university there. In the Habsburg lands Joseph II's last years witnessed a vigorous reaction against his programme of reform and centralization. His death in 1790 coincided with the seismic events west of the Rhine and left his successor, Leopold, doubly vulnerable to that embryonic national force which had been unleashed in France and by way of reaction to Joseph's enlightened absolutism in the Habsburg Empire too. Its impact on the growth of state power and on the relationship between state and subject was, of course, colossal, but such matters lie beyond the temporal confines of this work.

One final aspect of the *Aufklärung* deserves attention: its concern with history. The historians of the German Enlightenment differed in one crucial respect from their West European counterparts and that was in their attitude to religion. Whereas the *philosophes* tended to see the historical process as the freeing of mankind from religious domination, the German historians were fired with enthusiasm for man's religious drive. That enthusiasm had been stimulated by the development of pietism in late-seventeenth-century Germany. Pietism reflected the long-standing German preoccupation with individual freedom in interpreting the Bible, encouraging a distinction between the letter and the spirit. This distinction lay at the heart of *Aufklärung* history. In political terms it was revealed in the tension between the palpably inadequate social organizations which man had developed over time and his capacity for spiritual fulfilment. This latter quality was the liberating force which could help to reshape human institutions until they reflected rather more convincingly than contemporaries could allow, the free spirit of their architects. Hence the unwillingness of Schlözer and others to limit their analogies of the state to metaphors of the machine. For machines had no soul, no spirit by which to grow and develop.

For the historians of the German Enlightenment, therefore, freedom was not to be found in the distinctive liberties of corporate groups. Nor did they seek it in the rubble of a regime laid low in the name of a new kind of liberty. They sought it through the medium of history. They did not view history in the teleological fashion which, according to Carl Becker, distinguished and discredited British and French history writing of the Enlightenment. They did however share the *philosophes*' scorn for the approach of their common predecessors, whom von Schlözer called disdainfully, 'the Anno Domini men'.[46] The historians of the *Aufklärung* maintained that every age, though it formed part of the historical continuum, deserved to be judged in its own terms. Their relativism (which helps to explain why Montesquieu was the *Aufklärung's* favourite philosopher) is the key to their concept of history. For them liberty was not an attribute either to be safeguarded or spurned by the political order; it was an inherent element of it. That elusive quality of spiritual independence and striving which characterizes *homo sapiens* formed part of the *zeitgeist* of each historic age. It would reach its apotheosis only if some future state were to be 'animated by an ethical or spiritual ideal by which the inner life of man was enriched'.[47]

# REFERENCES AND NOTES

1. Norman Davies, *God's Playground*, 2 vols (Oxford 1981), I, pp. 159 ff.
2. *Ibid.*, I, pp. 279–80.
3. Jerzy Topolski, 'Sixteenth-century Poland and the turning point in European economic development', in *A Republic of Nobles*, ed. J. K. Fedorowicz *et al.* (Cambridge 1982), pp. 84–5.
4. The term *szlachta* refers to the Polish nobility as a whole, not simply to the lesser nobility or the gentry. See the asterisked comment in Davies, *op. cit.*, I, p. 206.
5. Davies, *op. cit.*, I, p. 218. Henryk Samsonowicz, 'Polish politics and society under the Jagiellonian monarchy', *A Republic of Nobles*, p. 61.
6. Perry Anderson, *Lineages of the Absolutist State* (London 1947), p. 284.
7. Davies, *op. cit.*, I, p. 340.
8. *Ibid.*, I, pp. 347–8.
9. Thomas Hobbes, *Leviathan*, Solar Press Facsimile of the London 1651 edn (Menston 1969), p. 62. Davies, *op. cit.*, I, pp. 350 ff.
10. Davies, *op. cit.*, I, pp. 287 ff.
11. Józef Andrzej Gierowski, 'The international position of Poland in the seventeenth and eighteenth centuries', *A Republic of Nobles*, p. 231.
12. Fedorowicz, *A Republic of Nobles*, p. XV.
13. Claes Peterson, *Peter the Great's Administrative and Judicial Reforms* (Stockholm 1979).
14. Michael Roberts, 'On Swedish history in general', *Essays in Swedish History* (London 1967 edn), p. 6.
15. On the argument about motivation for Swedish imperialism, see Michael Roberts, *The Swedish Imperial Experience, 1560–1718* (Cambridge 1979), pp. 3 ff.
16. Roberts, 'On aristocratic constitutionalism in Swedish history, 1520–1720', *Essays in Swedish History*, p. 20.
17. *Ibid.*, pp. 15–16.
18. *Ibid.*, p. 24. On the new absolutist symbolism introduced for Charles XII's coronation ceremony, see R. M. Hatton, *Charles XII of Sweden* (London 1968), pp. 78–81.

19. Roberts, 'Charles XI', *Essays in Swedish History*, pp. 242 ff. See too the essay by Kurt Ågren, 'The *reduktion*', in *Sweden's Age of Greatness, 1632–1718*, ed. Michael Roberts (London 1973), pp. 237–64.

20. Roberts, 'On Aristocratic constitutionalism', *op. cit.*, pp. 37–8.

21. Michael Roberts, *The Early Vasas: A History of Sweden, 1523–1611* (Cambridge 1968), p. 139.

22. Alf Åberg, 'The Swedish Army from Lutzen to Narva', *Sweden's Age of Greatness*, pp. 265 ff.

23. Ingvar Andersson, *A History of Sweden* (London 1956), p. 252.

24. Kurt Samuelsson, *From Great Power to Welfare State* (London 1968), p. 121.

25. *Ibid.*, pp. 119–20. Michael F. Metcalf, *Russia, England and Swedish Party Politics, 1762–1766* (Stockholm 1977), pp. 151–4.

26. Metcalf, *op. cit.*, p. 152.

27. Andersson, *op. cit.*, p. 275.

28. Michael Roberts, 'Great Britain and the Swedish revolution, 1772–3', *Essays in Swedish History*, p. 286.

29. Andersson, *op. cit.*, p. 295. Samuelsson, *op. cit.*, p. 125.

30. Michael Roberts, *Swedish and English Parliamentarism in the Eighteenth Century* (Belfast 1973), pp. 23–6. The author makes some thought-provoking observations on the threat posed by the *Riksdag* to the freedom of the individual in Sweden during the so-called Age of Liberty, pp. 34 ff.

31. For the background to the drawing up of the constitution, see Nils Stjernquist, 'The creation of the 1809 Constitution', in *Sweden's Development from Poverty to Affluence, 1750–1970*, ed. Steven Koblik (Minneapolis 1975), pp. 36 ff.

32. *Ibid.*, p. 60.

33. Hans Rosenberg, *Bureaucracy, Aristocracy and Autocracy: the Prussian experience, 1660–1815* (Cambridge, Mass. 1958), p. 31.

34. F. L. Carsten, *The Origins of Prussia* (Oxford 1954), pp. 179 ff.

35. Klaus Epstein, *The Genesis of German Conservatism* (Princeton 1966), pp. 396 ff.

36. Henri Brunschwig, *Enlightenment and Romanticism in Eighteenth Century Prussia* (Chicago 1974), p. 10. Immanuel Kant, *What is Enlightenment?* Kant on history, ed. L. W. Beck (New York 1963), p. 9.

37. Gerhard Oestreich, *Neostoicism and the Early Modern State* (Cambridge 1982), p. 46.

38. Epstein, *op. cit.*, p. 127.

39. Peter Hanns Reill, *The German Enlightenment and the Rise of Historicism* (Berkeley, Calif. 1975), p. 73.

40. *Ibid.*, pp. 138–9.

41. Leonard Krieger, *The German Idea of Freedom* (Boston 1957), p. 44.

42. Reill, *op. cit.*, p. 103.

43. Krieger, *op. cit.*, pp. 26–7, 38.

44. *Ibid.*, pp. 59 ff. The ideas and opinions of Thomasius are briefly summed up in Frederick Hertz, *The Development of the German Public Mind*, vol. 2: *The Age of Enlightenment* (London 1962), pp. 109–12.

45. Rosenberg, *op. cit.*, p. 191.
46. Reill, *op. cit.*, p. 35.
47. *Ibid.*, p. 217.

# CONCLUSION

Historians are sometimes accused of writing history which is of interest only to fellow historians. Such a reproach tends to ignore the fact that modern history writing is based upon the same principle as that which excited the historians of the eighteenth-century Enlightenment. We still stubbornly maintain that the political, social and economic problems which presently face mankind can only be understood, evaluated and resolved in an historical framework. This volume has been concerned with the application of that general principle to one of the crucial issues troubling the contemporary world, the nature of political freedom.

There are a number of conclusions to be drawn from our scrutiny of early modern Europe and of the eighteenth century in particular. The first is to reiterate Isaiah Berlin's judgment with which we began, that the concept of political freedom defies precise definition. It appears, not surprisingly, to assume forms dictated by particular political contours. Thus Britain's growing commercial hegemony led to the articulation of free-trade ideas which were acceptable to the men of property who both dominated the complex political order and were yet subject to it. It was feasible, therefore, for them to depict the pursuit of liberty in terms which neither suggested the imminence of anarchy nor the existence of entrenched despotic power. Such a strategy was not possible however in that other bastion of commercial freedom, the United Provinces. There a variety of wealthy urban and provincial groups clung tenaciously to their economic freedom resentful of any attempt by the House of Orange to curtail their liberties in order to preserve the Republic's security. That security was permanently threatened by the United Provinces' loss of commercial supremacy, and then the liberties of its patriciate took on the form of oligarchic privileges which were detrimental to the country's needs.

The situation in Poland was in most respects far removed from that of the Dutch Republic. The small northern Netherlands state clung uneasily to the coast of Western Europe, while the vast tracts of

Poland-Lithuania rolled majestically across Eastern Europe from the Baltic to the Ukraine. The Dutch Republic was urban-based, whereas in Poland towns had already lost their vitality by the time that the Dutch had acquired their independence. There was no monarchy and no serfdom in the United Provinces, nor was the Polish Commonwealth the centre of a world-wide trading empire. Yet the *szlachta*, like the Dutch regent class, possessed a set of liberties, originally based on commercial exploitation, which gave each of them the dominant voice in their respective country's affairs. The maintenance of those liberties became for the nobles of the Polish commonwealth, as for the burghers of the Dutch Republic, the supreme political objective. However, although each group was in a position to assert its liberties at the expense of the rest of the population, there was a counterfeit element in the one which was not to be found in the other. The Union of Utrecht established a republican form of government entirely consistent with the liberties which flowed from it. There was therefore a unity of form and spirit which was not present in the *Rzeczpospolita*. However that word is translated, whether as 'commonwealth' or 'republic', the Polish state was in fact a monarchy, but a monarchy taken over by its noble order.[1] The result was a tension between form and spirit which underlined the exclusive and absolute nature of Polish liberties, maintained at the expense of royal freedom of action on the one hand and peasant independence on the other.

Neither in Russia nor in Brandenburg-Prussia did noble freedoms so dominate the political order. In both these countries the nobility achieved success in establishing quite specific rights and spheres of influence, though firmly under the aegis of royal sovereignty. The possession of such clearly defined corporate freedoms inhibited the establishment of impersonal state authority which alone could spread liberty equally among all the subjects, or with equal even-handedness, remove it altogether. In this regard Russia and Brandenburg-Prussia were moving in opposite directions during the eighteenth century.

For a brief period Peter the Great threatened to transform old Muscovy into a regulatory regime demanding loyalty and service from all its subjects, including the tsar himself. Such a regime prefigured the modern state's characteristic requirement of equal subordination by the subjects to the sovereign will. The Russian political tradition which called for universal and abject submission to the will of the saintly tsar provided the inspiration for a secular alternative. Where there was no distinction between the public and private domain, there seemed to be an opportunity for the imposition of state autocracy. Peter's efforts at regulation and bureaucratization did not lead, however, to the emergence of the idea of the abstract state. Instead, they ushered in a regime of corporate liberties of the type which in the West, paradoxically, had long preceded rather than followed the evolution of that idea.

In Brandenburg-Prussia the Great Elector and his successors extended the area of public law but continued to respect the judicial authority of the provincial squires to whom they looked for administrative and military service. The Prussian bureaucracy had become a formidable organization by the time of Frederick the Great but it should be noted that even then the government's local officials *(landräte)*, besides representing the central government in the localities, were equally the custodians of the interests of the landed aristocracy in its dealings with government.[2] Nevertheless, the bureaucracy was assuming a status which made the emergence of impersonal statehood a conceivable possibility, even while Frederick's personal authority was paramount. When that autocratic figure left the scene, in 1786, the Prussian bureaucracy embraced their new role as 'servants of the state', a changed nomenclature which reflected 'the impact of fresh ideas, of novel concepts of public welfare and of allegiance in government service, and of more voluntaristic, and, therefore, more exacting standards of public ethics'.[3]

Besides, lodged deep in the Prussian polity was that germ of spiritual freedom offering the potential for an ideal public order in which alone each citizen could fully express his individuality. In the Prussian law code of 1794, which remained by and large a compilation of unequal rights based on estates, one general right was unequivocally proclaimed: 'Every inhabitant of the state must be granted complete freedom of religion and conscience.'[4] It was not surprising, therefore, that following the débâcle of 1806 Prussian reformers like Stein and Hardenberg should undermine the old junker exclusiveness, abolish serfdom and preach the gospel of the all-powerful state as the most secure haven of individual freedoms.

Spain resembled Brandenburg-Prussia in its combination of bureaucratic development and personalized kingship. Equally, in the motivating power of dynasticism it may be compared with France. Yet overall its development is not easily related to that of its European neighbours. The often crucial relationship between the noble order and the Crown was absent from eighteenth-century Spain. There the Crown had seized the high ground by its partial defeat of the provincial *fueros* – they remained intact throughout the period in Navarre and the Basque lands – so that it could dictate to the country at large from its central stronghold of Madrid. The lost liberties of the periphery, including commercial independence, had to be balanced against the liberating influence of a degree of common purpose. The rule of the Spanish Bourbons did not share the ambiguities which beset their French cousins. Theirs was an unfettered dynasticism which allowed them a greater freedom of action while continuing to inhibit the evolution of a new political order.

What, finally, of Sweden and France, where tensions between ideas of liberty and liberties created pressures for change that were more open and observable in the former, more subtle and concealed in the latter? In Sweden the effect of alternating regimes of monarchical absolutism and noble-dominated constitutionalism was to obscure the source of sovereignty sufficiently to encourage the eventual emergence of the idea of impersonal statehood presiding with equal authority over all subjects. In France the two strands were not revealed in separate forms of government but were present in the alternative inflexions of a single regime. So firmly tethered was French monarchy, however, by long-standing legal ties that it was quite unable to evolve either a more representative or more regulatory role. Consequently, even though the legal establishment spoke on occasion in terms of the citizens' universal liberty, the key to the *ancien régime* remained the sectional liberties of corporate groups. Therefore, the concept of the impersonal state failed to take root before the Revolution, though its appearance was foreshadowed in the writings of the *philosophes*. Rousseau, in particular, provided a significant stimulus by investing the state with a moral dimension, a development of crucial importance too in the thought of the German *Aufklärung*.

Rousseau started from the proposition that humanity's 'first law is that of self-preservation', and there can be no doubt that the growth of the power of central government sprang invariably from the threat of internal or external conflict. The speed at which that power was translated from a personal to an impersonal form seems to have depended upon the clarity with which it could be perceived. Where it lay hidden within the interstices of a complex political organization, the metamorphosis was quicker; where it was based upon clearly defined principles, the change was slow to take place. There were, of course, numerous gradations reflecting distinctive national or regional traditions. The veils of divine right kingship behind which Louis XIV and his successors sought to obscure the realities of government contributed with diminishing conviction to the idea that sovereign power in the French state might not be quite the same thing as dynastic absolutism. For a brief period it seemed rather more likely that the ill-defined but awesome power of the 'God-crowned' ruler of Muscovy might be transformed by the radical tsar Peter into the impersonal sovereignty of the state. However, in France the monarchy was defeated by the strength of its own traditional commitments. In Russia, Peter's hopes were dashed by the demystification of tsardom, leading to the unambiguous clauses of the Statute for the Administration of the Provinces and of the Charter of the Nobility, in which his successor, Catherine II, spelled out the terms upon which her sovereignty was based.

It certainly seems to have been the case that the idea of political liberty as a possession of all subjects acquired most vigour where the concept of the impersonal state loomed large, and developed with less force where it did not. That juxtaposition may be acounted for, of course, in terms of the individual's need to offset the unprecedented authority wielded by the modern state. The polarity of cossack and serf represents an unstable and extreme form of government in early modern Europe, yet in modified guises it may be widely applied. For in the most sophisticated political regimes, 'cossack' liberties depended upon 'serf' obligations. Liberty was an irrelevance in a political world based upon the inequality of relationships between government and governed. The fundamental insecurity of that world gradually dictated the emergence of the all-powerful state and with it a growing preoccupation with political liberty. That liberty is best perceived not as an antidote to state control but as an inherent aspect of state authority. It is perhaps more apparent in our own time than ever before that state security comes before individual liberty, that liberty indeed has no more meaning or relevance in an insecure regime than it had for the cossacks of the southern steppe or the serfs of Central and Eastern Europe. Although in the light of their different historical traditions, states may give more or less weight to the matter of political liberty, the fact is that for all of them freedom is ultimately a form of parole which they grant to their subjects to indicate a secure and untroubled polity.

Yet the received truth – at least in the West – is quite different. Habitually our emphasis has been on the freedom of the individual, while the power of the state has been relegated to the status of a necessary evil, to be invoked primarily when liberty is put at risk. Historically, developments went in quite the opposite direction. The responsibility for such a distortion has ironically to be levelled against those eighteenth-century historians who made the study of the past an indispensable guide to the present. Their preoccupation with human progress and development coincided with the decline of dynasticism and the hesitant appearance of the modern state idea. Later generations have found it difficult to separate the methodology of the new history from its content, so that eighteenth-century visions of freedom have become part of our historical heritage.

On a different level, the question arises of whether the desire for political freedom, being an altogether more noble aspiration than the craven pursuit of a secure subjection, should not always catch the historian's eye and be given the priority. Indeed, such a view coincides with the depiction of the state as a moral force, an idea already being promulgated in France and Germany and by Alexander Radishchev in Russia in the late eighteenth century. But in this matter the historian is moving to the very perimeter of his field, for he is not equipped to decide whether the perceived nobility of a particular attitude reflects an innate human trait or the conditioning of the age of reason. Carl Becker long ago reminded us of the danger of accepting the doctrines of the *philosophes* as statements of absolute truth. Whilst from his vantage point amongst them, David Hume cast his own philosophical doubts upon their faith in reason.[5] It should be added, however, that the overwhelming influence of Christianity in Western Europe for more than a millenium has made men uneasy about associating themselves publicly with the amoral code of *raison d'état* and readier to praise the individual's right to be treated justly.

In Eastern Europe the historians of the Enlightenment had less impact, quite naturally since they were not so widely known nor did their writings match the traditions of that region. Yet from the nineteenth century history was to become the supreme political mentor there too, as it already was in the West. Karl Marx was influenced by those German idealist philosophers and historians who saw man's ultimate spiritual fulfilment in the state. His interpretation of historical development led him from the world of economic exploitation in which he saw individuals as reflecting the collective and opposed outlooks of their class to the classless society where freedom meant total identification with the will of the community. Despite common intellectual roots, it was not a view calculated to sit easily with the alternative libertarian vision of Western Europe. But it was capable of adaptation to the Russian world of the commune and the autocrat. In the words of Nicholas Berdyaev,

> The old Russian monarchy rested upon an orthodox world outlook and insisted upon agreement with it. The new Russian State rests upon a world outlook and with a still greater degree of coercion requires agreement with it. The consecrated kingdom is always a dictatorship of a world outlook, always requires orthodoxy, always suppresses heretics. Totalitarianism, the demand for wholeness of faith as the basis of the kingdom, fits in with the deep religious and social instincts of the people.[6]

The battle lines, therefore, were drawn between irreconcilable ideologies based upon conflicting interpretations of the past. From the West it appears that the East has rediscovered serfdom; from the East that the West has revived the cossack cause. Neither perception, of course, does justice to the other side, and both serve to emphasize the gulf between them. However, in terms of the power of the impersonal state which underlies both positions, there is little to choose between them.

Whether we speak of freedom of expression or of belief, of economic or judicial freedom, of the right to vote or to form associations, the need for such rights to be universally available is of paramount importance if they are to be considered as aspects of political liberty. Citizens may not always possess the whole gamut of such rights; some may be allowed and others not. That in fact brings us back to the heart of the matter, namely, that political liberty, however defined or delimited, depends upon the state's willingness to permit its exercise. Only one freedom can claim absolute immunity from state control and that is the freedom of thought. Already by the closing decades of the eighteenth century the significance of that fact had dawned on enlightened minds as far apart as Edinburgh and St Petersburg. Adam Ferguson cautioned his readers in 1767 that

> Even political establishments, though they appear to be independent of the will and arbitration of men, cannot be relied on for the preservation of freedom; they may nourish, but should not supersede that firm and resolute spirit, with which the liberal mind is always prepared to resist indignities and to refer its safety to itself.[7]

A few years later, on the other side of the European continent, Alexander Radishchev quoted approvingly the words of J. G. von Herder, 'In the province of truth, in the kingdom of thought and spirit, no earthly power can or should pass judgment.'[8]

## REFERENCES AND NOTES

1.  *Rzeczpospolita* is derived from the Latin *respublica* and carries the same meaning.
2.  Rosenberg, *Bureaucracy, Aristocracy and Autocracy: the Prussian experience, 1660–1815* (Cambridge, Mass. 1958), p. 167.
3.  *Ibid.*, p. 191.
4.  Hajo Holborn, *A History of Modern Germany, 1648–1840* (London 1965), p. 274.
5.  David Hume, *A Treatise of Human Nature*, 2 vols (Everyman, London 1974 edn), I, pp. 168, 179.
6.  Nicholas Berdyaev, *The Origin of Russian Communism* (London 1937), p. 172.
7.  Adam Ferguson, *Essay on the History of Civil Society*, ed. Duncan Forbes (Edinburgh 1966), Part VI, Section V, p. 266.
8.  Radishchev, *A Journey from St. Petersburg to Moscow*, ed. R. P. Thaler (Cambridge, Mass. 1958), p. 165.

# BIBLIOGRAPHY

The themes of this book are not susceptible to a comprehensive or definitive bibliography. The following works are limited to those cited in the notes, arranged in a more accessible form.

## PRIMARY SOURCES

Argenson, René-Louis de Voyer de Paulmy, marquis d', *Considérations sur le gouvernement ancien et présent de la France*, Amsterdam 1764.

Argenson, René-Louis de Voyer de Paulmy, marquis d', *Journal et Mémoires*, ed. E. J. B. Rathéry, 9 vols, Paris 1859–67.

Bodin, Jean, *The Six Books of a Commonweal* (1576), trans. Richard Knolles and ed. K. D. McRae, Cambridge, Mass. 1962.

*Catherine the Great's Instruction (Nakaz) to the Legislative Commission*, 1767: vol.2 of Paul Dukes, *Russia under Catherine the Great*, Newtonville, Mass. 1977.

Condorcet, J. A. N. de Caritat, marquis de, *Esquisse d'un tableau historique des progrès de l'esprit humain* (1795), ed. M. and F. Hincker, Paris 1966.

Descartes, René, *Oeuvres*, eds C. Adam and P. Tannery, Paris 1964–65: *Discours de la Méthode* (1637); *Méditations* (1641)

Diderot, Denis (ed.), *Encyclopédie*, 17 vols, Neuchâtel 1765.

Fénelon, François Salignac de la Motte, *Examen de conscience sur les devoirs de la royauté*, printed in *Lettre à Louis XIV*, intr. Henri Guillemin, Neuchâtel 1961.

Ferguson, Adam, *Essay on the History of Civil Society* (1767), ed. Duncan Forbes, Edinburgh 1966.

Ferguson, Adam, *Principles of Moral and Political Science* (1792), 2 vols, Hildersheim 1975.

Flammermont, J., *Remonstrances du parlement de Paris au XVIII^e siècle*, 3 vols, Paris 1888–98.

Gibbon, Edward, *The Decline and Fall of the Roman Empire* (1776–88), ed. J. B. Bury, 7 vols, London 1909–14.

Hobbes, Thomas, *De Cive* (1642), New York 1949 ed.

Hobbes, Thomas, *Leviathan* (Scolar Press Facsimile of the London 1651 edn) Menston, 1969.

Hume, David, *History of England* (1754–62), 8 vols, Oxford, 1826.

Hume, David, *Of the Original Contract* (1748), printed in *Social Contract*, intr. E. Barker, Oxford 1971.

Hume, David, *A Treatise of Human Nature* (1739–40), 2 vols, Everyman, London 1974.

Kant, Immanuel, *What is Enlightenment ?* (1784): *Kant on History*, ed. L. W. Beck, New York 1963.

Karamzin, N. M., *Memoir on Ancient and Modern Russia* (1811), ed. Richard Pipes, Cambridge, Mass. 1959.

Law, John, *Oeuvres complètes*, ed. P. Harsin, 3 vols, Paris 1934: *Mémoire sur le denier royal* (1719); *Idée générale du nouveau système des finances* (1720).

Locke, John, *Two Treatises of Government* (1690), ed. P. Laslett, Cambridge 1960.

Locke, John, *Second Treatise on Civil Government* (1690), printed in *Social Contract*, intr. E. Barker, Oxford 1971.

Louis XIV: *Mémoires for the Instruction of the Dauphin* (1661–1668), ed. P. Sonnino, New York 1970.

Massillon, J. B., *Sermon pour l'Incarnation* (1718), *Oeuvres complètes*, 13 vols, Paris 1822–25.

Montesquieu, Charles-Louis de Secondat, baron de la Brède et de, *Oeuvres complètes*, ed. du Seuil, Paris 1964: *De l'esprit des lois* (1748).

Radishchev, A. N., *A Journey from St Petersburg to Moscow* (1790), ed. R. P. Thaler, Cambridge, Mass. 1958.

Robertson, William, *The Progress of Society in Europe* (1769), ed. F. Gilbert, Chicago 1972.

Rousseau, Jean-Jacques, *Discours sur l'origine et les fondements de l'inégalité parmi les hommes* (1755), Paris 1973.

Rousseau, Jean-Jacques, *The Social Contract* (1762), trans. G. Hopkins for *Social Contract*, intr. E. Barker, Oxford 1971.

Shcherbatov, M. M., *On the Corruption of Morals in Russia* (1786/87), ed. and trans. A. Lentin, Cambridge 1969.

Sieyès, Emmanuel Joseph, *What is the Third Estate ?* (1789), trans. M. Blondel, London 1963.

Smith, Adam, *An Enquiry into the Nature and Causes of the Wealth of Nations* (1776), ed. R. H. Campbell and A. S. Skinner, 2 vols, Oxford 1976.

Spinoza, B. de, *The Political Works*, ed. A. G. Wernham, Oxford 1958: *Tractatus Theologico-Politicus* (1670).

Temple, William, *Observations upon the United Provinces of the Netherlands*, London 1673.

*The Economics of A. R. J. Turgot*, ed. P. D. Groenewegen, The Hague 1977: 'In praise of Gournay' (1759); 'Plan for a Paper on taxation in general, on land taxes in particular, and on the project of a land register' (1763).

*Turgot on Progress, Sociology and Economics*, ed. Ronald L. Meek, Cambridge 1973.

Vico, Giambattista, *The New Science* (1744), ed. and trans. T. G. Bergin and M. H. Fisch, New York 1961.

Voltaire, François Marie Arouet, *Oeuvres historiques*, ed. R. Pomeau, Paris 1957; *Le Siècle de Louis XIV* (1751); *Précis du siècle de Louis XV* (1768).

Voltaire, François Marie Arouet, *Lettres philosophiques* (1734), ed. G. Lanson, 2 vols, Paris 1924.

Voltaire, François Marie Arouet, *La philosophie de l'histoire* (1765), ed. J. H. Brumfitt, Geneva 1969.

*Yermak's Campaign in Siberia* (16th–17th century Siberian chronicles), ed. Terence Armstrong, The Hakluyt Society, London 1975.

# SECONDARY SOURCES

Åberg, Alf, 'The Swedish Army from Lutzen to Narva', *Sweden's Age of Greatness*, ed. Michael Roberts, London 1973.

Ågren, Kurt, 'The *Reduktion*', *Sweden's Age of Greatness*, ed. Michael Roberts, London 1973.

Alexander, John, *Autocratic Politics in a National Crisis: the Imperial Russian Government and Pugachev's Revolt, 1773–1775*, Bloomington, Indiana 1969.

Añes, G., *El antiguo regime: los Borbones*, Madrid 1976.

Anderson, M. S., *Peter the Great*, London 1978.

Anderson, Perry, *Lineages of the Absolutist State*, London 1974.

Andersson, Ingvar, *A History of Sweden*, London 1956.

Antoine, Michel, *Le conseil du roi sous le règne de Louis XV*, Geneva 1970.

Antoine, Michel, *Le gouvernement et l'administration sous Louis XV*, Paris 1978.

Backus, Oswald P., 'Muscovite Legal Thought, the Law of Theft, and the Problem of Centralization, 1497–1589', *Essays in Russian History*, ed. A. D. Ferguson and A. Levin, Hamden 1964.

Baker, K. M., *Condorcet*, Chicago 1975.

Baudrillart, A., *Philippe V et la cour de France*, 5 vols, Paris 1890–1901.

Becker, Carl L., *The Heavenly City of the Eighteenth-Century Philosophers*, Yale 1960 edn.

Berdyaev, Nicolas, *The Origins of Russian Communism*, London 1937.

Berlin, Isaiah, *Four Essays on Liberty*, Oxford 1969.

Berlin, Isaiah, *Vico and Herder*, London 1976.

Blum, Jerome, *Lord and Peasant in Russia from the Ninth to the Nineteenth Century*, Athaneum edn, New York 1964.

Bogoslavkii, M. M., *Oblastnaya reforma Petra velikogo*, Moscow 1902.

Bonney, Richard, *Political Change in France under Richelieu and Mazarin, 1624–1661*, Oxford 1978.

Bordes, M., 'Les intendants éclairés de la fin de l'ancien régime', *Revue d'histoire économique et sociale*, **39** (1961).

Bosher, J. F., *French Finances, 1770–1795*, Cambridge 1970.

Brooke, John, *The House of Commons, 1754–1790*, Oxford 1964

Brunschwig, Henri, *Enlightenment and Romanticism in Eighteenth-Century Prussia*, Chicago 1974.

Bury, J. B., *The Idea of Progress*, London 1928.

Bush, Michael, *Noble Privilege*, Manchester 1983.

Butterfield, *The Whig Interpretation of History*, London 1931.

Callahan, W. J., *Honor, Commerce and Industry in Eighteenth-Century Spain*, Harvard 1972.

Caponigri, A. R., *Time and Idea. The Theory of History in Giambattista Vico*, London 1953.

Carr, Raymond, *Spain, 1808–1939*, Oxford 1966.

131

Carsten, F. L., *The Origins of Prussia*, Oxford 1954.

Cherniavsky, Michael, *Tsar and People*, New York 1961.

Church, Clive H., *Revolution and Red Tape: the French Ministerial Bureaucracy, 1770–1850*, Oxford 1981.

Church, William F., *Richelieu and Reason of State*, Princeton 1972.

Cobban, A. B., *In Search of Humanity*, London 1960.

Cracraft, James, *The Church Reforms of Peter the Great*, London 1971.

Croce, B., *History as the Story of Liberty*, London 1941.

Cross, A. G. (ed.), *Russia under Western Eyes, 1517–1825*, London 1971.

Davies, Norman, *God's Playground*, 2 vols, Oxford 1981.

Desdevises du Dézert, G., 'Les institutions de l'Espagne au XVIIIe siècle', *Revue Hispanique*, **70** (1927).

Dickson, P. G. M., *The Financial Revolution in England*, London 1967.

Doyle, W., 'The parlements of France and the breakdown of the old regime, 1771–1788', *French Historical Studies*, **6** (1970).

Doyle, W., 'Was there an aristocratic reaction in pre-revolutionary France ?', *Past and Present*, **57** (1972).

Duke, Paul, *Catherine the Great and the Russian Nobility*, Cambridge 1967.

Dyson, Kenneth, *The State Tradition in Western Europe*, Oxford 1980.

Egret, Jean, *Louis XV et l'opposition parlementaire*, Paris 1970.

Egret, Jean, *La pré-révolution française, 1787–1788*, Paris 1962.

Elliot, J. H., *Richelieu and Olivares*, Cambridge 1984.

Epstein, Klaus, *The Genesis of German Conservatism*, Princeton 1966.

Esper, Thomas, 'The Odnodvortsy and the Russian nobility', *Slavonic and East European Review*, **45** (1967).

Fedorowicz, J. K. *et al.* (eds), *A Republic of Nobles*, Cambridge 1982.

Fedosov, I. A., 'Sotsial'naya sushchnost' i evolyutsiya rossiyskogo absolyutizma', *Voprosy Istorii*, **7** (1971).

Forbes, Duncan, 'Sceptical Whiggism, commerce and liberty', *Essays on Adam Smith*, eds A. S. Skinner and T. Wilson.

Gierowski, Jozef Andrzej, 'The international position of Poland in the seventeenth and eighteenth centuries', in *A Republic of Nobles*, ed. J. K. Fedorowicz.

Gleason, W. J., *Moral Idealists, Bureaucracy and Catherine the Great*, New Brunswick, New Jersey 1981.

Gossman, L., *The Empire Unpossess'd: An Essay on Gibbon's 'Decline and Fall'*, Cambridge 1981.

Greengrass, Mark, *France in the Age of Henri IV*, London 1984.

Gruder, Viven R., *The Royal Provincial Intendants: a Governing Elite in Eighteenth-Century France*, Ithaca 1968.

Haddock, B. A., *An Introduction to Historical Thought*, London 1980.

Hanley, Sarah, *The Lit de Justice of the Kings of France*, Princeton 1983.

Hargreaves-Mawdsley, W. N. (ed.), *Spain under the Bourbons, 1700–1833*, London 1973.

Hatton, Ragnhild M. and Bromley J. S. (eds), *William III and Louis XIV: Essays by and for Mark A. Thomson*, Liverpool 1968.

Hatton, Ragnhild M., *Charles XII of Sweden*, London 1968.

Hatton, Ragnhild M., 'Louis XIV and his fellow monarchs', in *Louis XIV and the Craft of Kingship*, ed. John C. Rule.

Hazard, P., *La crise de la conscience européenne*, 3 vols, Paris 1935.

Herr, Richard, *The Eighteenth-Century Revolution in Spain*, Princeton 1955.

Hertz, Frederick, *The Development of the German Public Mind*, vol. 2: *The Age of Enlightenment*, London 1962.

Hexter, J. H., 'The birth of modern freedom', *Times Literary Supplement*, 21 Jan 1983.

Holborn, Hajo, *A History of Modern Germany, 1648–1840*, London 1965.

Holmes, G. S., *Augustan England. Professions, State and Society, 1680–1730*, London 1982.

Huppert, G., *The Idea of Perfect History: Historical Erudition and Historical Philosophy in Renaissance France*, Illinois 1969.

Jones, Robert E., *The Emancipation of the Russian Nobility, 1762–1785*, Princeton 1973.

Kamen, Henry, 'El establecimiento de los Intendentes en la adminstracion española', *Hispania*, **95** (1964).

Kamen, Henry, 'Melchor de Macanaz and the foundations of Bourbon power in spain', *English Historical Review*, **317** (1965).

Kamen, Henry, *The War of Succession in Spain, 1700–15*, London 1969.

Kaplan, S. L., *Bread, Politics and Political Economy in the Reign of Louis XV*, 2 vols, The Hague 1976.

Keens-Soper, H. M. A., 'The French political academy, 1712: a school for ambassadors', *European Studies Review*, **2** (1972).

Keep, J. L. H., 'The Muscovite elite and the approach to pluralism', *Slavonic and East European Review*, **48** (1970).

Kelley, D. R., *Foundations of Modern Historical Scholarship*, New York 1970.

Kennedy, William, *English Taxation, 1640–1799*, London 1964.

Kerhane, Nannerl O., *Philosophy and the State in France*, Princeton 1980.

Klaits, Joseph, 'Men of letters and political reform in France at the end of the reign of Louis XIV: the founding of the Académie Politique', *Journal of Modern History*, **43** (1971).

Klaits, Joseph, *Printed Propaganda under Louis XIV*, Princeton 1976.

Koenigsberger, H. G. 'The organisation of revolutionary parties in France and the Netherlands during the sixteenth century', *Journal of Modern History*, **27** (1955).

Kossmann, E. H., 'The development of Dutch political theory in the seventeenth century', in *Britain and the Netherlands*, eds J. S. Bromley and E. H. Kossmann, London 1960.

Kossmann, E. H., 'The crisis of the Dutch State, 1780–1813: Nationalism, federalism, unitarism', in *Britain and the Netherlands*, IV, eds J. S. Bromley and E. H. Kossmann, The Hague 1971.

Krieger, Leonard, *The German Ideas of Freedom*, Boston 1957.

Lanier, L., 'Le club de l'entresol (1723–1731)', *Mémoires de l'académie des sciences, des lettres et des arts d'Amiens*, 3ème série, **6** (1879).

Lemaire, A., *Les lois fondamentales de la monarchie française*, Paris 1907.

Leyden, W. van, *Hobbes and Locke: the Politics of Freedom and Obligation*, London 1981.

Lloyd, Howell A., *The State, France and the Sixteenth Century*, London 1983.

Longworth, Philip, *The Cossacks*, London 1969.

Macfarlane, Alan, *The Origins of English Individualism*, Oxford 1978.

Macpherson, C. B., *The Political Theory of Possessive Individualism: Hobbes to Locke*, Oxford 1962.

Madariaga, Isobel de, *Russia in the Age of Catherine the Great*, London 1981.

Man'kov, A. G., *Ulozhenie 1649 goda*, Leningrad 1980.

Mann, F. A., 'Outlines of a history of expropriation', *The Law Quarterly Review*, **75** (1959).

Meehan-Waters, Brenda, *Autocracy and Aristocracy: the Russian Service Elite of 1730*, New Brunswick 1982.

Metcalf, Michael F., *Russia, England and Swedish Party Politics, 1762–1766*, Stockholm 1977.

Momigliano, A., 'Gibbon's contribution to Historical Method', *Historia*, 2 (1954).

Mousnier, Roland E., *Les XVI^e et XVII^e siècles*, Paris 1961.

Mousnier, Roland E., 'L'évolutions des institutions monarchiques en France et ses relations avec l'état social', *Le dix-septième siècle*, 57–59 (1963).

Mousnier, Roland E., *The Institutions of France under the Absolute Monarchy, 1598–1789*, vol. 1: *Society and the State*, London 1979.

Mousnier, Roland E., *The Institutions of France under the Absolute Monarchy, 1598–1789*, vol. 2: *The Organs of State and Society*, London, 1984.

Munsche, P. B., *Gentlemen and Poachers: the English Game Laws, 1671–1831*, Cambridge 1981.

Namier, L. B., *The Structure of Politics at the Accession of George III*, 2 vols, London 1929.

Noel, C. C., 'Opposition to enlightened reforms in Spain: campomanes and the clergy, 1765–1775', *Societas*, **3** (1973).

Oestreich, Gerhard, *Neostoicism and the Early Modern State*, Cambridge 1982.

Ortiz, A. Dominguez, *Sociedad y estado en el siglo XVIII español*, Madrid 1976.

Parker, David, 'Law, society and the state in the thought of Jean Bodin', *History of Political Thought*, **II** (2), 1981.

Peterson, Claes, *Peter the Great's Administrative and Judicial Reforms*, Stockholm 1979.

Pipes, Richard, *Russia under the Old Regime*, London 1977 edn.

Plumb, J. H., *The Growth of Political Stability in England, 1675–1725*, London 1967.

Pompa, L., *Vico, a Study of the New Science*, Cambridge 1975.

Rabb, Theodore, K., *The Stuggle for Stability in Early Modern Europe*, Oxford 1975.

Raeff, Marc, *The Origins of the Russian Intelligentsia: the Eighteenth Century Nobility*, New York 1966.

Raeff, Marc, *Plans for Political Reform in Imperial Russia, 1730–1905*, Englewood Cliffs, New Jersey 1966.

Raeff, Marc, 'The Enlightenment in Russia and Russian thought in the Enlightenment', *The Eighteenth Century in Russia*, ed. J. G. Garrard, Oxford 1973.

Raeff, Marc, 'The well-ordered police state and the development of modernity in seventeenth- and eighteenth-century Europe: an attempt at a comparative approach', *American Historical Review*, **80** (1975).

Ranum, Orest, *Artisans of Glory: Writers and Historical Thought in Seventeenth-Century France*, North Carolina 1980.

Ranum, Orest and Patricia (eds), *The Century of Louis XIV*, London 1973.

Reill, Peter Hanns, *The German Enlightenment and the Rise of Historicism*, Berkeley, California 1975.

Renier, G. J., *The Dutch Nation*, London 1944.

Roberts, Michael, *Essays in Swedish History*, London 1967 edn.

Roberts, Michael, *The Early Vasas: a History of Sweden, 1523–1611*, Cambridge 1968.

Roberts, Michael (ed.), *Sweden's Age of Greatness, 1632–1718*, London 1973.

Roberts, Michael, *Swedish and English Parliamentarism in the Eighteenth Century*, Belfast 1973.

Roberts, Michael, *The Swedish Imperial Experience, 1560–1718*, Cambridge 1979.

Rodríguez, Laura, 'The Spanish Riots of 1766', *Past and Present*, **59** (1973).

Rogger, Hans, *National Consciousness in Eighteenth-Century Russia*, Cambridge, Mass. 1960.

Rosenberg, Hans, *Bureaucracy, Aristocracy and Autocracy: the Prussian Experience 1660–1815*, Cambridge, Mass. 1958.

Rothkrug, Lionel, *Opposition to Louis XIV: the Political and Social Origins of the French Enlightenment*, Princeton 1965.

Rowen, Herbert H., *The King's State: Proprietary Dynasticism in Early Modern France*, New Brunswick 1980.

Rule, John C., 'King and Minister: Louis XIV and Colbert de Torcy', in *William III and Louis XIV*, eds Ragnhild M. Hatton and J. S. Bromley, Liverpool 1968.

Rule, John C. (ed.), *Louis XIV and the Craft of Kingship*, Ohio 1969.

Salmon, J. H. M., 'The Paris Sixteen, 1584–94: the social analysis of a revolutionary movement', *Journal of Modern History*, **44** (1972).

Samsonowicz, Henryk, 'Polish politics and society under the Jagiellonian monarchy', *A Republic of Nobles*, ed. J. K. Fedorowicz

Samuelsson, Kurt, *From Great Power to Welfare State*, London 1968.

Sarrailh, Jean, *L'Espagne éclairée de la seconde moitié du XVIII<sup>e</sup> siècle*, Paris 1954.

Schama, S., *Patriots and Liberators: Revolution in the Netherlands, 1780–1813*, London 1977.

Shennan, J. H., *The Origins of the Modern European State, 1450–1725*, London 1974.

Shennan, J. H., *Philippe, Duke of Orléans: Regent of France, 1715–1723*, London 1979.

Shennan, J. H., 'The political vocabulary of the parlement of Paris in the eighteenth century', *Atti del quarto congresso internazionale della società italiana di storia del diritto*, Florence 1982.

Skinner, A. S., 'Adam Smith: an economic interpretation of history', *Essays on Adam Smith*, eds A. S. Skinner and T. Wilson, Oxford 1975.

Skinner, A. S. and Wilson, T. (eds), *Essays on Adam Smith*, Oxford 1975.

Skinner, Quentin, *The Foundations of Modern Political Thought*, 2 vols, Cambridge 1978.

Stewart, J. H., *A Documentary Survey of the French Revolution*, New York 1951.

Stjernquist, Nils, 'The creation of the 1809 constitution', *Sweden's Development from Poverty to Affluence, 1750–1970*, ed. Steven Koblik, Minneapolis 1975.

Stradling, R. A., *Europe and the Decline of Spain*, London 1981.

Taylor, George V, 'Noncapitalist wealth and the origins of the French Revolution', *American Historical Review*, 72 (1967).

Thompson, E. P., 'The moral economy of the English crowd in the eighteenth century', *Past and Present*, 50 (1971).

Thompson, E. P., *Whigs and Hunters*, London 1975.

Topolski, Jerzy, 'Sixteenth-century Poland and the turning point in European economic development', *A Republic of Nobles*, ed. J. K. Fedorowicz.

Trevor-Roper, Hugh, 'The historical philosophy of the Enlightenment', *Studies on Voltaire and the Eighteenth Century*, 27 (1963).

Troistky, S. M., *Russky absolyutizm i dvoryanstvo b XVII b.*, Moscow 1974.

Vernadsky, G. *et al* (eds), *A Source Book for Russian History from Early Times to 1917*, 3 vols, London 1972.

Vicens Vives, J., *Approaches to the History of Spain*, Berkeley, California 1970 edn.

Wallerstein, Immanuel, *The Modern World System*, vol. 2: *Mercantilism and the Consolidation of the European World Economy, 1600–1750*, London 1980.

Wansink, H., 'Holland and six allies: the Republic of the Seven United Provinces', in *Britain and the Netherlands*, IV, eds J. S. Bromley and E. H. Kossmann, The Hague 1971.

White, R. J., *The Anti-Philosophers*, London 1970.

Yaney, G. L., *The Sytematization of Russian Government: Social Development in the Domestic Administration of Imperial Russia, 1711–1905*, Urbana 1973.

# INDEX